OYEZ! OYEZ! OYEZ!

THE STORY OF A TOWN CRIER

F. Tregarthen Gibson
(Town Crier of Exmouth, Devon)

Author of
Exmouth - Her Age of Elegance

HALSGROVE

First published in Great Britain in 2005

British Library Cataloguing-in-Publication Data
A CIP record for this title is available from the British Library

1 84114 486 X

HALSGROVE

Halsgrove House
Lower Moor Way
Tiverton, Devon EX16 6SS
Tel: 01884 243242
Fax: 01884 243325
email sales@halsgrove.com
website www.halsgrove.com

Printed and bound in Great Britain by
CPI Bath

PREFACE

It gives me great pleasure to be asked to write the preface to this book. I was intrigued by the accuracy and research that the author must have gone to to collate the information that has been included.

As Chairman of the Ancient and Honourable Guild of Town Criers, a former Councillor and Town Mayor of Nailsworth in Gloucestershire, I found myself relating to so many of the experiences the author brings to these pages. I have enjoyed reading the story of his life – and of the life of a Town Crier – which I am sure his readers will also enjoy.

Anthony (Tony) Evans
Chairman
Ancient & Honourable Guild of Town Criers

TONY EVANS
INTERNATIONAL TOWN CRIER

'Larhone'
24 Box Crescent
Minchinhampton
Gloucesterhire
England GL6 9DJ
01453 731355

The Ancient and Honourable Guild of Town Criers was formed at a meeting held at Hastings in 1978. The aims of the Guild are to foster goodwill and friendship among all Town Criers and to safeguard them in their ancient calling.

MY THANKS

There are so many to be thanked! First, my family who have given me the time and encouragement to continue writing instead of playing five-a-side football, even seven-a-side rugby! None more so than the advice Marjorie, my wife of over fifty years has given me. In practical terms Joanne, our granddaughter and William who assisted in translating the Cornish into English on a disk for onward transmission. They have also been responsible for the photographic section and for those photographs they have not taken themselves, for arranging the inclusion of other photographers who have contributed. Without their help and specialist know-how none of this would have been possible - a superb team. I am grateful also to the President, Bill Malin (Alcester), and Chairman, Tony Evans (Nailsworth) of the Ancient and Honourable Guild of Town Criers for their invaluable contributions.

Thanks too, to the five Mayors for the privilege of sharing their company over the years, including two Lady Mayors who in that capacity have made my life even more enjoyable. To John Wokersien, the Town Clerk and all the team in the Town Hall my sincere thanks for all your help and assistance. Our choice of living in Exmouth I share with Marjorie, but I have been fortunate indeed to have a group of people with whom, due to their quality status have made 'my fifth retirement' such pleasure. Thanks.

My thanks to all in the largest town in Devon; to each and every one of the 34,000 for your encouragement, smiles and wherever possible your efforts to make Exmouth an even more pleasant place in which to work and live. There is still much to do.

I look forward to working with my third Lady Mayor and write this on the eve of her appointment together with the Lady Deputy. We can only repeat the pledge 'There is much to do', and I am hoping to be included in the team in May 2006.

I am delighted yet again to be associated with Halsgrove, in particular Simon Butler, The Publisher, and his team who have been so helpful.

My thanks to you all.

J. Tregarthen Gibson

Town Crier of Exmouth
November 2005

CONTENTS

Oyez! Oyez! Oyez! The author in full cry.

INTRODUCTION
The Past, Present and Future

A publisher friend, as we all do, was obviously looking for work when he questioned me about a book on Town Criers. In my haste to avoid the next question, I quickly suggested that there must be many in print at the moment. Surprise, surprise! I did nothing about it! He did! And the question I was trying to avoid was raised – 'Why don't you?'. At the time I knew little about the crying game but strangely enough when I made enquiries myself I found little information. Town Criers, themselves were perhaps too busy getting on with the practical side of their occupation. Libraries and a few historians were not aware of any great activity in recording the lives of the Town Crier. Meagre enthusiasm and dearth of information were apparent. The modern method of recording information, on the internet, is scarce, certainly on national and international Town Criers. Nevertheless there are some individual attempts at ensuring that my Home Town is connected to the necessary surf of their own environment. Equally, there are a few Criers who had some time to put pen to paper, or is it now ink to tape? Or online? In order to regale us with their lives in livery I am personally grateful to my colleagues in this respect and have acknowledged their contribution in the text. My own experiences are recorded as it happened. Accurately, I trust, but maybe with a little, if not poetic, then licence in another form which is included in the life story accompanied, inevitably through imagination and dreaming.

The peace and quiet at home, enabling one to concentrate has much to commend it, but the motivation to sit and scribble has to be organised. Research is obviously necessary, perhaps the recording of it is essential if only to avoid the difficulty of memory, or is it recall? Sometimes, to be kind to the afflicted, it becomes a senior moment! Unfortunately, when the failures are stacked up the recall procedure becomes time-consuming and writing slows, finally stops – one hopes not forever, yet! Get on! Enjoy! Keep working! In a recent editorial in *The Crier*, Tony Evans, Chairman of the Ancient and Honourable Guild of Town Criers wrote: 'Your unique experiences as Town Criers will almost certainly be of interest to others.' Challenged by the Chairman, I have made my response! No excuse on offer!

Obviously writing is personal. Views vary. Interpretation of certain situations differ. Methods of compiling facts are sometimes far apart. Sources are widely distributed. Conclusion, being a summary of all the differences, makes individual views interesting, but still views are seen through the eyes, thought, aspirations of one particular person. I would wish that these individual feelings be aired. There is much contained in this document which can be seen as representing common practice. These are usually the more formal activities. The variation on how they are tackled is instanced, for example, in competition. The Crier is asked to first base their first cry on 'my home town'. The difference becomes obvious, because of the fact that towns do differ. How then to ensure that my cry is the best? And this is answered by the judges who look for inflection, colour, pauses, emphasis and originality in the delivery of the facts. Even the number of words is not identical, somewhere between 75 and 100. I had thought of asking every Crier to send me their home cry to contribute to the whole story. But second thoughts told me to hold back, it was a colossal enterprise if ever the host of Town Criers responded. Nevertheless, the interest in many of these traditions can only be handed on if contributions to the story are encouraged. I have found a lasting and fascinating interest in the lives of others and look forward to my colleagues entering into competition with each other, adding something of their own life to that of others. Contributions would be welcome - the Editor of *The Crier* would be delighted. So, I hope, would be the Chairman. I certainly would welcome additional comments and views.

My immediate task is to identify the sources of information. I have somewhere in the text made reference to *Bells and Yells: the Town Crier's Story* written by Robert Tremain from Launceston (the Cornish get everywhere!). But I am grateful to him for opening up many different avenues of hidden history and interesting news and views on Town Criers. Did you know for example, that an extinct civic office 'the Mayors wait', i.e. waiting and watching at the town's gates and walls, calling the hours of their watch, the time of curfew and the number of occasions of opening and closing of the gates, was part of the Criers job description? No, neither did I, but I did find 16 references in the bible that clarify the situation and answered the question. Thank you to the writers, scholars of biblical times, in addition to Robert who also tells me that fairs and meetings were proclaimed – there is a carving in stone in the porch of St Thomas in Launceston of a figure of a man blowing a trumpet – the forerunner of the bellman or Town Crier, and that the Parish Church of Bishop's Hull in Somerset contains a 16th century carved bench end of similar note. Purely from memory, now hidden in the years that have passed, I vaguely remember or to be accurate, recall, that there is a church in Zennor that has a number of carved pew ends. One that is of a magnificent mermaid, a real significance in this context! However, I think that she has attracted sailors and here my memory fails completely; but do visit Zennor in West Cornwall sometime and find out.

Somewhere I have mentioned the formidable part played by Devonshire in providing a crowd, a gaggle, a bevy, and a multitude certainly of Town Criers. In some cases, their tasks vary. For example Honiton has a Glove Fair, Exeter a Lammas Fair, Barnstaple a St Giles Fair, whilst Kingsbridge celebrates a late July Fair dating from 1461 granted by a charter from the Abbot of Buckfast. Dates vary throughout, not only in Devon, but also in the British Isles. Holsworthy, to mention another in this county, is given as 11th century, while 12th and 13th century fairs are mentioned in historical archives. There is a Town Crier recorded in Marlborough in 1204, Norwich in 1272.

However, there are common denominators. One, almost routine, occurs in May in Exmouth, and the other I hope to establish in the near future before the town grows to such a size that I will unfortunately be unable to walk to distance: 'Beating the Bounds'! The annual proclamation 'Oyez! Oyez! Oyez! All manner of persons here present are requested to keep silent while the necessary proceedings of the Council are being taken for the election of the Mayor for the ensuing year. God save the Queen.' I trust very soon, perhaps on any sunny day this summer (it always shines in Exmouth), that I can declare that the ancient rites and customs of the beating of the boundaries of Exmouth have been carried out and completed, 'We, the Mayor and assembled company are pleased to report that all is well and the boundaries of this, our beloved town are secure. God save the Queen'.

Another May, another Mayor. It is a well loved tradition and I for one enjoy the celebration and taking a small part in the festivities. But will there be another Lady Mayor elected? Who knows?

F. Tregarthen Gibson
Exmouth 2005

The author in full 'International Cry'. This is a rare photograph taken 'in action' at the 10th World Town Criers Championship held in Newquay, Cornwall on 13-17 May 2003.

*Exmouth's coat of arms and (below) as worn on the right
shoulder of the author's regalia. See Appendix 1 for the full story.*

1

THE TOWN CRIER OF EXMOUTH

The *Concise Oxford Dictionary* describes a 'Town' as (i) a large urban area with a name, defined boundaries and local government, being larger than a village and usually not created a city. (ii) any densely populated area, especially as opposed to the country suburbs. (iii) the people of a town ('the whole town knows of it') (iv) the chief town in one's neighbourhood ('went up to town') (v) the central business in shopping area in the neighbourhood (just going into town) (vi) the permanent residents of a university town as distinct from the members of the university. Uses of the word include: 'to 'go to town' – act or work with energy and enthusiasm; 'on the town' – enjoying the entertainments, especially the nightlife of the town – celebrating; 'Town Clerk' – the officer of the corporation of a town in charge of records and administration, the secretary and legal advisers of a town corporation until 1974; 'Town Council' – the elective governing body in a municipality; 'Town Councillor' – an elected member of this, usually resides in the 'Town Hall' – a building for the administration of local government having public meeting rooms; 'Town Mayor' – the chairman of a Town Council; 'Town Meeting' – a meeting of the voters of a town for the transaction of public business, such as town planning, the planning of the constructions and growth of towns. A 'Townie' – a person living in a town, especially as opposed to a countryman or (in a university town) a student. 'Townsfolk', 'Townspeople' – the public of a town.

Do you know, and perhaps you will agree that the above comfortably describes Exmouth? Certainly as far as the citizens are concerned. Again that statement needs, if not clarification, then expansion. But, these dictionary statements make no mention of the Town Crier. An omission some would say. Not all towns or cities have the office. There happens to be one such in Exmouth, so, perhaps this is the spot which lights up the Town Crier of Exmouth.

THE CRIER/CRYER
A person who cries:
An officer who makes public announcements in a court of justice. A town or

OYEZ! OYEZ! OYEZ!

Common Crier – an officer employed by a town council or local authority to make public announcements in the streets or market place. A 'cri de coeur' – a passionate appeal complement or protest (French, cry from the heart).

This statement from the *Concise Oxford Dictionary* is, of necessity, concise. It is worth an explanation.

What are the qualities of a good Crier? 'Sustained volume and clarity, pitch and inflection and dignity' Here are some who qualify.

If you were asked to name a career that could take you around the world, the chances are that a town crier would not be the profession that immediately springs to mind. Yet for Bromyard town crier Peter Dauncey, that's exactly what has happened. His job has taken him to the likes of Singapore, Australia and Bermuda.

It was in 1994 that Peter first took up the traditional bell and tricorn hat. He was present at a meeting of the local tourist group and was asked for ideas to brighten up the town. 'I suggested a town crier and a spring festival and, as luck would have it, I ended up as the town crier and the chairman of the festival!' he said.

Peter's inspiration came from a trip to Truro in Cornwall, where he saw a crier attracting big crowds. A good start to a career! He is a former chairman of the Ancient and Honourable Guild of Town Criers.

Peter's first costume had to be hired, before he eventually had one made by a tailor in Bristol. 'It's worth £3,000 and was made from leftovers from costumes for TV programmes,' he explained. Peter's costume is a copy of a senior warrant officer's uniform from around 1740, when criers were traditionally retired military men. Before that, the history of town crying is blurred. 'No one knows when the first crier was appointed but the first recorded one is on the Bayeux Tapestry,' said Peter. 'William the Conqueror was a great reformist and a great radical and he wanted his new laws spread throughout the land in the local dialect.' (from *Malvern Gazette* – Phil Tromans).

2

WELCOME TO EXMOUTH

Coaches arrive from many parts of the country and indeed from overseas to enjoy our wonderful town with its heritage coastline and landscape. The passengers disembark outside the hotel of their choice to take up residence for a prescribed period of time; I am often asked to meet the groups to welcome them to Exmouth and sometimes to join them in entertainment organised for them in their hotel. On one such occasion, I was asked to board the coach to meet the passengers at the invitation of the manager on their arrival at the hotel. They were comfortably ensconced in their seats. I regaled them of the exquisite venue they had selected for their holiday. I briefly outlined the highlights of the town. Their visit included historic and architectural features and the events that were about to take place in the near future to coincide with their stay. I further congratulated them on choosing such a popular and very helpful hotel manager and staff. I assured them that he would arrange, indeed, rearrange, mealtimes to provide them the opportunity of joining in the activities in the town and an unforgettable holiday in Exmouth.

On the beach at Exmouth, chatting with summer visitors during the notable Annual Sand Sculpture Competition.

During the course of this preamble an elderly lady, who was looking some-what distressed, finally managed to lift herself from the seat in which she had been fidgeting. She pronounced quite clearly that they knew all that. They had been here on holiday for the last week and were about to leave for home! Amid much laughter and applause which then receded, she announced 'and we met you in the centre of the town and heard all about it; you haven't forgotten have you? To which there was only one reply, 'Bon Voyage, we will meet again next year'. And to complete the circle, some did, including another friend now christened 'Assistant Town Crier' from Newcastle upon Tyne, who returned with his wife to holiday in Exmouth. The manager thought it was a huge joke and fortunately so did all concerned including me!

It is an increasing part of my role, just meeting people, which I enjoy doing. In fact, encouraging them to return again and again to share in that which we are fortunate to have in abundance here for Devon. Kind, helpful peo-ple. Individuals who smile. To offer a special welcome. Engage in conver-sation. Giving up time to share with others who are genuinely thankful for the traditions of county and seaside life, often handed down from genera-tion to generation. Locals, always mindful of their origin, are sincere, kind-ly, generous in time and take pleasure in association. Friendly, often to the point of over indulgence. Proud people. Proud of their inheritance. And what's more, willing to share it with others. That's Exmouth!

But things change, tradition wavers. People are placed in precarious positions. It becomes more difficult to uphold beliefs. But while there are people who politely propose passionately that the position is permanent, like the one passenger, we will continue 'The Welcome To Exmouth' com-munication.

Other more sombre moments come to mind. The Crier's activities, Mayor Making, the Civic Service; perhaps serious or not so sombre; dignity, dressed up in regalia and appearance before the populace. Ceremonies to go through in a prescribed form and format. There is a quiet subdued and con-trolled atmosphere at these ceremonies.

There is a change in tone, tune and activity for example, when opening a fête or fair usually for a charity when I have been known to dance with the Lady Mayor and Deputies, to sing with the congregation and to offer clues to the next speaker who occasionally forgets the routine.

I am equally guilty of such lack of recall, known these days, as a 'senior

moment'. The memory lives on, but recalling incidents is sometimes difficult. Mainly, my routine is thoroughly enjoyable. Certainly it is varied, often busy, and frequently very busy. Part of the routine is the weekly 'shout' (Routine?) at midday on Saturdays from the Magnolia Centre, the pivot of the town. However it can clash with events in other parts of the locality. Somehow the information made available to me over the weekend finds its way in the forecast and is included early in the following week. The routine is important to those who listen, demand it, those new to it, especially visitors who enjoy the informal ceremony, and sometimes applaud. Those who haven't yet heard the proclamation will have to wait patiently for the repeat.

Top: Mayor Making. New Mayor, new Deputy, new Town Crier.
Above: Every second Wednesday in the month the Farmers' Market comes to Exmouth and is welcomed.

3

COMMUNICATION
IS THE NAME OF THE EXERCISE

The first appointments of Town Criers in this country came following the Norman Conquest. William the Conqueror, through the Act of Winchester, decreed that all large cities and towns should have a crier to spread the news, warn of danger, and other important happenings, throughout the kingdom. With illiteracy high amongst the populace the crier took on the role of a 'talking newspaper', giving proclamations, edicts and laws, besides the news. Their common cry of 'Oyez!, Oyez!, Oyez!' roughly translated means 'hark' or 'listen'. Many great events in history would been have announced this way.

The historical role has been continued, and today the main function of the Town Crier is to actively promote tourism, town events, civic occasions, charitable events and business. The position and role of Town Crier is carried out today in over 150 cities, towns and unitary authorities, throughout England and Wales. It's is not exclusive to these shores either; many other countries throughout the world including Australia, New Zealand, America, Canada, South Africa, Bermuda and some European countries, have Town Criers.

Members of The Loyal Company and of the Ancient and Honourable Guild of Town Criers (AHGTC) have strict codes of practice to which Criers have to adhere. To apply for membership, the Crier has to be appointed and minuted by his Town or City Council, or a Lord of the Manor, who will be required to sign the Criers application form to join in the Guild as proof of his or her appointment.

The robes or regalia of the Crier are usually traditional to the Town. Some choose to relate to a period of historical dress important to their town.

SUMMARY OF THE ROLE OF TOWN CRIER – AN AMBASSADOR

Mayor making ceremonies and in council.
Introductions at Civic Events in town and environs.

Announcing forthcoming events in the community.
Greeting Representatives – visitors and guests.
Remembrance and other inter-denominational Services.
Town Events, celebrations, Christmas lights, the festival of Exmouth.
Town Crier contests, gatherings to promote tourism – The carnivals.
Promoting the town at other Town Gatherings to visitors.
Charity events and businesses.

There are, at the time of writing, about 190 Town Criers in Britain, some throughout Europe and a few around the world. They represent towns, cities and in some cases the Lords of the Manor. Often the latter were absorbed into another community, usually as the population grew in nearby towns. The history of town crying is blurred. One says, quite accurately, although there are other claims, that the first recorded one is depicted in the Bayeux Tapestry. Others say William the Conqueror was a great reformist and radical and he wanted his laws spread throughout the land in the local dialect. In Shakespeare's time, another would say, the office achieved its peak in numbers. Those who have studied biblical history point to the Old Testament. Mention is made in historical circles that in Roman Britain Town Criers were messengers, fleet of foot, who would travel between settlements, bringing news of battles. The bad news for these unfortunates was, in those days, that bearers of bad tidings would often be put to death.

There was a need to communicate in their way of life at that time. From the Middle Ages until the end of the nineteenth century Town Criers were an established part of life. When the majority could not read they were the only way for the information to be disseminated to the public. They would also sound the alarm in case of fire or theft, or invasion of privacy.

Criers were an extension of the system of King's Messengers and as such were representatives of the monarch, and would always end their messages with 'God Save the King' or 'Queen'. They read from a scroll, subsequently fixed to a wooden post, performing the function of newspapers. As literacy spread, their role was eventually superseded by the regular press, many of whose worthy publications were named after those very posts as in the *Yorkshire Post*.

Highlights of international as well as national news, including threat of war, the death of a sovereign or a member of the Royal family and proclamations of births and marriages were included. Local events taking place either seasonally or annually were listed and even 'lost and found' items were added to the criers shout. Death is always present, and announcement of deaths became the forerunner of the obituary column. The 'media' as it is known today and the publishers of newspapers appeared and took over the role of spreading information.

The 'media' expanded. Newspapers, magazines, radio, TV are in everyday common usage, so very different from the three criers in Chester who worked on the shift system in the 16th century. The busy city also employed a night bellman who announced the time by hours and was empowered to be a look-out for those breaking the curfew. Tourism, a 20th century activity, encouraged people to travel further afield and cleared the approach for an increase in those promoting trips and longer holidays. A new era was born. Not only on road and rail, but aircraft which took larger and larger numbers of travellers on journeys. The town through its criers responded. Instead of the once a week 'shout' (noon appealed as a suitable hour), it became every day and finally seasonal (which because the weather dictated, meant April to September).

Town crying has seen a resurgence in recent years. There are many more in Devonshire than any other county and I am very fortunate to be one of that august company. Many historic towns like Exmouth use their own crier for ceremonial purposes, official openings and civic events. Then there are the competitions. My eye was first caught by the following:

The new Town Crier
OYEZ – OYEZ – OYEZ
EXMOUTH TOWN CRYER COMPETITION
Saturday 21st September 1996
MAGNOLIA CENTRE – EXMOUTH
At 1 o'clock of the hour
EXMOUTH'S FIRST TOWN CRIER
OF THE NEW EXMOUTH TOWN COUNCIL

Application forms and further information
available from Exmouth Town Hall.

This was my first introduction to the office of the Town Crier. Soon after this notice was posted in and around Exmouth the successful candidate was carrying out his duties in the town. I had heard him, which is a necessary qualification for the holder of the appointment! I had attended the Mayor's Ball where the appointee acted as Master of Ceremonies. In addition I had witnessed the newly appointed Town Crier, in full regalia carrying out his other duties within the town. A tower of strength. He had contested the compe-

18

tition, triumphed over all, and with the good nature with which he was endowed, plus his infectious smile, had made his mark on the new position he had been offered. His name? Nathaniel Bradley. He was a well-known Master Baker and was responsible with his wife for running a most popular establishment in the town, and although now retired is seen in and around Exmouth, taking an interest in what is happening with his usual smile on his face. Nat, as he is known, made a most valuable contribution to the life of the town and is to be congratulated on his endeavours. I, personally, have never been involved in running a business of any kind, and would not have had the temerity to attempt that for which Nat was well known. Just imagine – rising at 4am – baking until the opening of the shop – selling until closing – doing the accounts – preparing for the next day – living a life – falling into bed – falling out into the bakery – to start all over again!

Nat was the Exmouth Town Crier but found it increasingly difficult to cope, with his already full life as a baker. Ultimately, he had to reconsider his position and somewhat reluctantly had to resign! He has, as I have indicated, since retired, having now more time to relax and enjoy his new lifestyle. Good luck to you and yours, Nat.

The repercussions of how to fill the void and to find someone to carry out the duties and responsibilities so ably carried out by Nat was the inevitable result of his retirement as Town Crier.

I had been much involved with the restoration of the house in which my wife and I had purchased a flat, along with twelve other apartment owners. In addition to the work on a house of great historical interest I was in the middle of researching a book on the previous owners of Dolforgan Court, and resisted all attempts to lure me away from my completion of that work. That book is now published and the following chapter provides a summary of the publication from one of the reviews.

An award - not only for visiting, but also for painting, although it was for children!

4

EXMOUTH - HER AGE OF ELEGANCE
A NEW BOOK REVIEWED

Garth, or to use the author's full name Tregarthen Gibson is a present day resident of Dolforgan Court where he lives with his wife Marjorie. He has used his research on the history of that house and one of its previous occupants to create a fascinating picture of Exmouth during its Victorian and Edwardian hey-day.

The founder of the first hospital in Exmouth was Mrs Anna Charlotte Hume-Long who lived and died in 1899 in Dolforgan. In 1884 she started the Maud Hospital in Clarence Road, which rapidly became too small. She then pur-chased two properties at the top of Bicton Street to house the Maud Hospital and the Hope Orphanage both of which she was a matron and benefactor. On her death in 1899, her son added to her legacy, which subse-quently created the Exmouth Hospital, the foundation stone being laid in 1902.

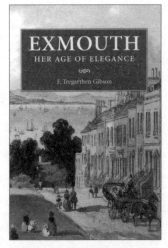

The front cover of Exmouth - Her Age of Elegance.

Dolforgan Court in 1875 was the lavish establishment of Mrs Hume-Long, the wife of an M.P. and mother of two more, both of whom were elevated to the peerage. She, her-self, although not titled attained the local name of 'Lady Bountiful', on account of her charita-ble works in and around Exmouth. There were ten children, five girls and five boys in the family, two of whom gave their names to the original orphanage and hospital.

The book is an interesting record of her life from 1875 when she arrived in Exmouth taken from records of that time and as the title indicates during the period of the Age of Elegance.

The author became interested in Dolforgan, an imposing elegant building that is now divided into thirteen flats in Louisa Terrace. As a Director of the Management Company, formed in 1987, the agreed stated aim of all the residents was 'to restore the mansion to its former glory'. The fascinating life of the era 1850–1900 unfolds, including the life of the nineteen servants employed. The story takes the reader across a thousand years and the development of Exmouth through that period. There is a great deal of history to dip into here and anyone with an interest in the town will find a great deal to enjoy.

Garth is now The Town Crier of Exmouth. History continues! Born in St Just in Penwith, Tregarthen is a proud Cornishman. Educated at Cape Cornwall Primary School, later at Penzance County School for Boys (now Humphrey Davy) and after a period overseas in His Majesty's Service, he rejoined what is now Loughborough University. He taught in many different types of schools throughout the country, retiring in 1985 as an Inspector of Schools. A family man with children and grandchildren, he enjoys life, particularly his role as Town Crier and keeps himself occupied as a member who participates in the life of the community of Exmouth.

The book *Exmouth - Her Age of Elegance* is published by Halsgrove of Tiverton and is on sale locally as is distributed widely.

* * *

As a postcript to the previous chapter, and to use a rather flippant quote from the 'Good Book' – 'and the Lot fell on' Tregarthen. I am pleased to confirm that Nathaniel was appointed Town Crier for the town of Exmouth and was confirmed at a meeting of Exmouth Town Council held on Monday 14 October 1996.

Copy of a reference from Doug Fletcher – then the Crier of Topsham.

To the Committee of the A.H.G.T.C.
Gentlemen & Ladies,
Let it be proclaimed that I give my wholehearted approval that Mr. N. Bradley is very suitable to be the Town Crier of Exmouth of which he is a good citizen, having interviewed him a few times.

Yours truly,

D. Fletcher
15 October 1996

5

MEMBERSHIP OF THE ANCIENT AND HONOURABLE GUILD OF TOWN CRIERS

Membership of The Ancient and Honourable Guild of Town Criers is dependent upon a local authority appointing applicants to the office of Town Crier. Should you be accepted into the Guild you are expected to swear an oath of allegiance to Her Majesty The Queen and to The Guild as well as the Office of Town Crier. I had previously done so to the King – in His Majesty's Service. One Nathaniel Bradley was appointed in 1996 and retired soon after. Then came Tregarthen.

Shakespeare provides two references pertinent to the theme of my appointment. In *Twelfth Night.* Mavolio in cross garters (which I do not wear): Act 3 Scene 4: 'Some are born great, some achieve greatness – some have greatness thrust upon them'.

And relating to The Town Crier in *Hamlet* :

Act 3, Scene 2 – A hall in the castle – Hamlet and certain players - Hamlet speaks: 'Speak the speech, I pray you, as I pronounced it to you, trippingly on the tongue; but if you mouth, as many of your players do, I had as lief the town crier spoke my lines.' He continues with his lesson to the players.

Continuing this theatrical theme I herewith present Characters and Players in the appointment of the new Town Crier in the new Millennium in the Town Hall, Exmouth. Cast in no particular order:

A NEW PLAY- NEW MILLENNIUM - 2000

Councillor Brenda Taylor	Mayor of Exmouth 1998 to 2000
Councillor John Taylor	Consort to the Mayor (husband of Brenda and now a Councillor himself)
Councillor Graham Kirby	Who was mainly responsible for the appointment of the Town Crier of Exmouth – one Nathaniel Bradley.

Nathaniel Bradley

Appointed on Monday 14 October 1996, resigned 1999, the Mayor at the time being Councillor Geoff Chamberlain and handing over accoutrements to Francis Tregarthen Gibson, 2000.

Councillor Ron Mudge

Elected Mayor of Exmouth 8 May 2000

Councillor Pat Graham

Deputy Mayor appointed on 8 May 2000.

Town Clerk – John Wokersien Town Hall Exmouth always in attendance.

All those Councillors named above and others have, from time to time, endeavoured to persuade me to volunteer for the office of The Town Crier, none more so than Brenda and John, Ron and Graham. Finally they won! I gave in, partly due to the fact that in a lecture arranged by Exmouth Society entitled 'The New Millennium' (given in Holy Trinity Church by Robin Bush a former Archivist in Somerset), I was encouraged to continue. 'Don't stop doing things because you're getting old or poorly, you'll stop soon enough if and when you do get older or poorly.' So! Here I was, ever onward to 2000 and beyond. Finally, it is a non-political post and I am anxious to help others, to share with everyone in Exmouth the joys of living in a delightful part, not only of this country, but of the world. I had also lodged my book on Exmouth for proofreading with the printers and someone had that information. As I had no defence, I agreed acceptance.

THE CEREMONY

Annual Council Procedural Note – 8 May 2000.

Town Crier leads the Mayor into the Chamber. He will enter, stop, ring the bell and say 'Please be upstanding to receive the Mayor of Exmouth, Councillor Mrs Brenda Taylor' Then he leads the Mayor to her chair.

Outgoing Mayor 'takes the chair' wearing robes.

The Mayor invites Reverend Gillespie of Tower Street Methodist Church to say a prayer.

The Mayor opens the meeting by welcoming The Chairman of the County Council, Chairman of The District Council and Distinguished Guests, fellow councillors and members of the public. Opens the meeting with a few words

23

to say 'that this is the Annual Council meeting and therefore my last meeting in this office. I would like to take this opportunity to say how much I have enjoyed my term of office' – and continues to address the Council.

Apologies Taken.

Election of Mayor:
Mayor asks Councillor Cope to propose the election of the Mayor and he will make a short speech.

Mayor asks Councillor M. Mitchell to second the proposition and delivers a short speech.

Mayor then puts the proposition to the vote asking for all those in favour, any against.

Then Mayor declares Councillor Ron Mudge elected as Mayor until the next Annual Meeting in the year 2001.

The new Mayor changes seats with the retiring Mayor.

Election of Deputy Mayor
New Mayor asks Councillor Ron Roberts to propose the appointment of the Deputy Mayor and makes a short speech.

Mayor asks Councillor Joe Freeman to second the proposition and a short speech.

Mayor then puts the proposition to the vote asking for all those in favour and any against.

The Mayor declares Councillor Pat Graham elected as Deputy Mayor

Adjournment
The Mayor then declares a short adjournment to allow the retiring Mayor, the Mayor and Deputy Mayor to leave the chamber to don their robes and to allow the press to take photographs.

Councillors Ron Mudge and Pat Graham then don the robes in the Committee Room and don chains of office. The retiring Mayor returns to the Council Chamber. The Town Crier leads the Mayor and Deputy Mayor into the Council Chamber. On entering he stops, rings the bell and declares,

'Please be upstanding and receive Councillor Ron Mudge the Mayor of Exmouth and Councillor Pat Graham the Deputy Mayor of Exmouth' and takes his place in the Council Chamber.

Declarations of Acceptance of Office
The Mayor then reads the declaration of acceptance of office and signs it.

The new Mayor will then make a speech in praise of the retiring Mayor and presents her with a past Mayor's badge and make a few comments about what he sees as the main priorities for the year ahead.

The Mayor then invites the Deputy Mayor to read her declaration of acceptance of office and to sign it.

The Deputy Mayor then makes her acceptance speech.

The rest of the business follows, as on the agenda.

One of the duties of New Mayor is to appoint the Town Crier, which is carried out with ritual simplicity. The newly appointed Town Crier will respond and in customary fashion will accept the office.

Acceptance
Mr Mayor, Madame Deputy Mayor, Councillors, Friends.

I have the honour, and I trust, for you, it is a great pleasure, to have another Town Crier, following in the footsteps of my able predecessor, Nathaniel Bradley. Can I thank those who have cajoled, bullied and used painless means, to encourage me, to undertake, this very necessary, and interesting role?

I trust, that with your help, co-operation and kindness, I may contribute, to the continuance of progress, in all its forms, in our splendid town of Exmouth.

May I, especially thank, Councillors Brenda and John Taylor, Councillor Graham Kirby, the Town Clerk and his staff, for all their powers of persuasion in promoting, the position of the Town Crier.

I trust that I will be able to assist, both the Deputy Mayor and The Mayor, in their duties, as well as carrying out those of the Town Crier.

Thank you – everyone

And removing my tricorn hat pronounce '*God Save The Queen*' and that's how it happened!

Why?

You may well ask, after all those formalities of a Town Crier. I had no intention of committing myself to a 'timetable', which had controlled or influenced my working life. I wished now that I had time to do all the things that previously I had no time to attempt. Nevertheless, I am, basically timetabled for many of the events I attend. I am programmed some years ahead and that information is relayed to me by an efficient team within the Town Hall, led by the Town Clerk.

The arrangement is that I can in fact, do as much or as little as I can manage. Initially that suited me and within the office of the Town Clerk I could attend this or that function, celebration, event or meeting(s) I found useful in promoting Exmouth town.

Duties and Responsibilities of the Town Crier

1. Those which the Mayor, through the Town Clerk and Secretary, wish me to carry out. Similarly with the Deputy.
2. Those which Member of Town Council, Chair of Councillors nominate through the Town Clerk that I can help and assist.
3. Those requested either through the office or by personal contact, which if linked with Exmouth qualify for promotion. The whole of the present development of the Town, through the Town Manager, the Forum, and the Working Parties to enhance Exmouth occupies much time of elected members, staff and me!
4. Finally, the duties of the Town Crier involve taking care of the Mayor

All is voluntary; that is unpaid. Although if a contribution is made, it is usually paid into the Mayor's Fund for local Charities or sometimes a particular one, for example The Friends of Exmouth Hospital who benefit from contributions received. Latterly, in dealing with Voluntary Bodies, I sometimes ask if they would nominate a Charity of their choice and any fees are passed on in that way. I have participated in the Exmouth Festival, which has developed, as always, from an interesting starting point and is now an attractive spectacle. Yet to be enacted is the ceremony of Beating the Bounds. This takes on an ever-widening area of the development of the town as the maps over 100 years old shows quite clearly. It is an ever-increasing ring of concentric concrete circles encircling the boundaries. Maybe it should be checked and marked by the old custom, if only to ensure its continuance as an historic event, and to involve the inhabitants of the far flung 'Empire of

Exmouth'. It is difficult, I find, to pinpoint the exact centre of these delightful satellites around the periphery of the town. No pub, no community centre, no provision for child's play and no plinth for the Town Crier to use on which to shout. Small shopping areas have to suffice in addition to the 'Shout' in the Magnolia Centre usually at noon on Saturday, if one is able to do so, despite other commitments.

After my inauguration ceremony, congratulations abound. I find that volunteers are often met with acclamation, and very complimentary remarks were passed as to my 'looking the part'. Much of that approval was derived from the Town Criers robes. All the necessary accoutrements were provided through the generosity of Exmouth residents. First in the order of precedent was Councillor Rotarian Graham Kirby. He and his wife, Shirley, presented the very fine medallion inscribed on the back, or reverse, side: 'Presented to Exmouth Town Council, October 1996', and the medallion bears the coat of arms of the town. I am grateful to the first appointed crier, my able predecessor, Nathaniel Bradley who cared for and added to the original regalia.

Where would we, male Town Criers be, without the ladies? That's not a sexist remark. There are Lady Town Criers! My long-suffering, yet understanding wife of 52 plus years, now called an Escort, encouraged me to participate and for her pains had to stitch me into the uniformed robes. 'Not the first time he's been stitched up' I overheard one or two comments! There were a few alterations to be made. Did you know for example, some of you may have experienced it, one foot is often larger or smaller than the other!? Without going into too many details, there were several parts of my anatomy that had to be changed, that is the robes and robing had to be altered. White stockings, some wear tights! Not cross-gartered as in Shakespeare's day, worn by Malvolio in *Twelfth Night*, but nevertheless they, the tights, were recognised as I walked through the streets to my first Council Meeting. Or was it the legs? Or more specifically the calves? It was suggested on that balmy evening, hiding in the shadows 'Someone's wife uses Persil!' The length of both legs encased in breeches or pantaloons, brought the comment 'a fine pair of calves' which I overheard without any reference to my having nothing to do with farming! Head shrinking took place, but on the night it all worked.

I am grateful to the suppliers in Exmouth from whatever source for the pleasure I have in wearing the vestments of office. Many of the groups have by various means festooned my uniform with examples of their considerable expertise, and the results are there for all to see, bringing many comments upon the extreme care taken to produce the finished product. The coat of arms for Exmouth leads the decoration in advance of many other embroidered features.

It seems an appropriate moment to add to my personal thanks to those who have helped and assisted me in undertaking this interesting position in the community. I enjoy wearing my regalia as I do with a great deal of pride. I am merely the coat-hanger on which the following have displayed their skills.

Tribute to 'The Ladies of the Wardrobe'
From an article in the *Exmouth Journal* on Thursday 17 January 2002 including a photograph of the Town Crier, yours truly, with the hard working ladies who are responsible for his ceremonial dress. They are included in the following report:

> *The Queen may have her own 'Mistress of the Wardrobe' but Exmouth's Town Crier has his own 'Ladies of the Wardrobe'. The ladies, who have been responsible for dressing the crier, Garth Gibson, in his finery, were at Monday night's meeting of Exmouth Town Council so that their work could be acknowledged.*

> *The meeting also provided an ideal opportunity to show the council a new Honiton lace jabot that had been specially hand made by Margaret Leese. The jabot was started last year and has taken 400 hours to complete. It is highly decorated and depicts scenes of Exmouth and the magnolia Grandiflora Exmouthensis.*

> *The other hard-working ladies include Hilary Higgins, who was Garth's first contact with the embroiderers team, and was responsible for the initial organisation.*

> *Ann Stredwick, from the Exmouth Women's Institute, a practitioner in embroidery, was responsible for the Exmouth coat of arms and Jean Haynes, from the Exmouth and Devon Embroiderers, researched and planned both the badges of East Devon District Council and the grandiflora Exmouthensis for the tricorn.*

> *Enid Floyd, Chair of the Exmouth Afternoon Townswomen's Guild, was responsible for the Devon county badge and the crest and coat of arms of Devon. Lillian Trivet and Yvonne Hinds were also present, as was David Fletcher, who presented a badge in his capacity as president of the Lions Club of Exmouth.*

Chair and Devon coordinator of the West Country Embroiderers, Mary Cron, who embroidered the badge of the Ancient and Honourable Guild of Town Criers, was unable to attend the presentation as she was in Spain.

Garth said: 'I am privileged as the Town Crier of Exmouth to wear such regalia and I do so with pride.'

In addition to those who participated initially using their considerable expertise in embroidery and lace-making there have been presentations from the members of the Exmouth Rotarians and Exmouth Amateur Rowing Association who, not to be forgotten, have taken some space on the colourful collar cape worn with the regalia.

A special 'thank you' is to be recorded in acknowledgement of considerable intricate work in providing the Town and Crier with additional civic regalia including selected materials to represent Exmouth. Sara Radford, of Cottesloe Brides, has produced period clothes of 1709, the uniform for a gentleman of the early 18th century. The delightfully chosen blue material represents the sea of Exmouth while the gold trimmings reflects the sand. All is constructed in period with care, with the buttons, buckles and bows used to increase the delight experienced by the many who have admired the costume. So, too, have independent judges at Town Criers' Competitions throughout Devon, and Exmouth's Town Crier has won 'Best Dressed' on several occasions, a triumph for those concerned, a reward for them and the town and all who contribute to colour and tradition in Exmouth.

30th December 2002

Garth,

You may recall our conversation in the Magnolia Centre this morning, concerning your 'red feather' and the Cornish connection with the 46th Foot. I thought you might be interested in the following extract from the official guide in the Regimental Museum at Bodmin.

'The Battle Of Paoli – 1777 American War of Independence

On the night of 20 September 1777 a British Force which included the Light Company of the 46th Foot surprised an American detachment under General Wayne, killing and capturing 400 Americans with a loss to themselves of only 8 killed and wounded. The Americans vowed they would give no quarter to the British troops engaged. Units concerned in the attack dyed their white hat feathers red in order that they might be more easily identified in the future. This is the origin of the red backing to the cap badge of today. In former years, imitation red feathers formed part of the headdress badge.

In 1782 the 46th became the 46th (South Devonshire) Regiment and in 1881 were amalgamated with the 32nd Foot and became 2nd Battalion Duke of Cornwall's Light Infantry.'

I am grateful to Brian Parker of the Royal British Legion, Exmouth for this very informative reminder of the ancestral colouring in my tricorn hat.

Before closing the tribute to the ladies of Exmouth there are a few comments that are very relevant. The period which the Exmouth Town Crier costume represents is either early 18th century or even 17th. The items worn today eminently copy and are based on original fashions. Research is a profitable occupation but time-consuming accuracy is necessary, and hunting to find the desired pieces quite exhausting. However, there is a place known to many of us who revere Exmouth's historical and architectural heritage – Exmouth Museum – from which so much help in maintaining our tradition comes. A set of lace cuffs? A jabot? And always someone, perhaps the curator's wife, will manufacture Magnolia Grandiflora Exmouthiensis overnight. Both curator and wife head a team of volunteers/friends of the museum, who, over a long period of time have enthralled a great number of people who have visited 'our museum'. Meanwhile the Curator finds time to write the following on Exmouth's history.

Lace for a Queen

The year 2002 has been chosen by 'OIDFA' (organisation Internationale de la Dentelle au Fuseau et a le Aiguille 1982) an international organisations relating to the making hand made bobbin and needle lace. This year the Congress is to be held in Nottingham on August 15 and 18. Lace makers will come from all over the world to take part. Competitions and workshops will be held over a few days and prizes will be awarded to those judged to be the best. Exhibitions will also take place locally in Honiton and Sidmouth Museums and during the Festival of Exmouth.

It had been thought for some time that the Huguenots were responsible for introducing Honiton Lace into Devon, when they came here in the 17th century, escaping from religious persecution in their own country. However research has found evidence of a local lace being made before their arrival. Called a 'Bone Lace' or trolley lace. No doubt over a period of time the two styles of bobbin lace merged into what we have today. In the 17th century over 4,000 people were employed in East Devon in lace manufacture. A slump came towards the end of the 18th century when lace went out of fashion in favour of muslin and gauzes. And to make matters worse in 1810 they were successful in making net Nottingham by machinery, which reduced the price and time factor of lace making.

Trade picked up again in 1840 when Queen Victoria asked to have wedding dress made in Honiton Lace but it never regained its former popularity and towards the end of the 1800s over 20 lace schools in Exmouth were closed down. The pupils of the Lace School did receive some basic education but their main occupation was to produce lace. At one time there were approximately 300 lace makers in Exmouth, mostly living in the Fire street area and there were many shops and manufacturers who would purchase the finished lace from those who made it. They in turn sent it via Honiton to London and other centres and it is suggested that is how the local lace came to be 'Honiton Lace'.

The Honiton Lace industry has been fortunate in having the patronage of members of the Royal Family over the years. Queen Victoria ordered a black lace shawl in silk made with sprigs of Honiton Lace mounted on the machine made net. On the occasion of the Coronation of King George VI and Queen Elizabeth, a Honiton Lace fan was presented to the Queen by the people of Honiton and a handkerchief was made for her in 1939. Our present to the Queen as Princess Elizabeth was given a lace-mounted Cocktail Tray as a 21st birthday gift.

Lace making today, caries on as a hobby and classes are arranged under the banner of further education. Several years ago the Speaker of the House of Commons was presented with a lace jabot, which he wears with his robes of office. Recently the Exmouth Town Crier was also presented with a lace jabot, which depicts the Grandiflora Emouthiensis Magnolia and the clock tower of Exmouth. Both Jabots have recently been at a lace exhibition in Nottingham.'

* * *

Whenever I am asked to give one of my talks to a society or group I usually start by thanking those who have contributed to the elegant regalia I wear. Originally inherited from my predecessor and now with the new civic uniform I describe my apparel, starting at the head and terminating at my feet.

Interestingly enough my tricorn hat is adorned according to the activity of the group with whom I am involved. I attended a wedding recently as the

Devon lace makers, photographed in the late nineteenth century. Above left: Mrs Long, Harry Whiddon and Mrs Horn with their lace makers pillows. Above right: Harry Whiddon with two elderly lace makers.

M.C. and the bride insisted that I wore a sprig of rosemary in my tricorn hat. It is the recipient of poppies in November and for Cornwall it overflows with coloured feathers. A gold cover over the crown suffices for celebrations and plain black for usual attire. My badge of office hangs from a golden sash and proudly presents a gold medal, given by a former Councillor who started the search for a Town Crier in 1996.

White tights/stockings, sometimes two pairs in bitter weather, recede into black shoes with designer buckles. A toff, some say, and a variety of comments meet the bearer, but none is so welcome as the children whose wish is sometimes granted, if they ask politely, 'Can I ring your bell, sir?' This, in its turn, encourages them to question why? And particularly at Carnival they shout Oyez! Oyez! I do have a school of young criers, who look forward to seeing me drawn by reindeer, not in green or blue, but in seasonal red. Not too difficult to discern. Even Santa has to have a holiday sometimes and, if anyone is confused, he is usually to be seen in Exmouth during the Summer enjoying a break from the cold frozen North. A man of many parts and one for all seasons. But what's the motivation – making history?

6

THE FAMILY TREE OF THE TOWN CRIERS

In my unending search into the Family Tree of the Town Criers of Exmouth, I came across a print of the turn of the century 1900–1920. It was enclosed in a magazine covered in dust, but nevertheless was of interest to me. It was headed 'Jolly Whiddon, Town Crier of Back Street'. The street was one of many that have now, through development, disappeared. Some of them had a water pump operated by hand, usually at the end of a cul-de-sac. When in such a position in Exmouth, with your back to the wall and surrounded on all sides, you look for a note about the prints which assisted me to identify Harry. The lace makers seen in the sepia print opposite are Mrs Horne, Harry Whiddon, the Town Crier, and Mrs Long who died at her home in Fore Street. The picture was taken in late 19th century, early 20th century. In 1917 the year in which her third grandson was killed in action in the Great War, Mrs Long was 92. This little window into the past is very precious. A well-designed footstool, so necessary for the work she carried out sits on her lap. In this case although most of the world outside would call it Honiton lace, it would, of course be Exmouth Lace and made by Exmouthians from Back and Fore Street in fact. Their dress is typical of the period, their white aprons, and they would be white, boiled and boiled again before being bleached in the bountiful back yard bath in brilliant sunshine.

The workstand, puff or cushion, was part of the lace makers essential equipment. Manufactured for the individual to ensure comfort and composure for the worker in lace. John with cap and waistcoat, the ladies in bonnets stop to have their picture taken – see opposite. They in that era were always working, tirelessly, normally for the family. But how they must have felt for the loss of yet another young man far away in the field of conflict.

Harry is heavily moustached as was the custom and no doubt as Town Crier. But more of him later. On his left is Mrs Horne, as E.R. Delderfield recalled, 'another' grand old Exmouth figure'. She was one of a band of Exmouth makers of Honiton Lace who combined to make the Coronation dress for Queen Mary.

The search now moves north to Bristol and to Mrs E.V. Burton, niece of the late Mr and Mrs William Crang and cousin of their four sons and two daughters. Charlotte Ethel, mother of the Crang sisters and their four brothers, was the third daughter of Mrs Long and married William Crang, a Brixham man and a great character.

To illustrate this 'one off' resident of Brixham, it is said of him, that he sold fish at prices that would make a fish diet extremely popular today. All his customers regarded him as a friend. It was well known and seriously stated that he went back to Brixham to get his haircut. Everybody knew him and loved him during the long years of his sojourn in Exmouth, to which he probably came in the first place for work, as did so many others.

Tragedy was nothing new in the Long family. It came to them when the boy and four girls were small. They lost their father, a master builder and architect. There were no craft guilds, homes for the destitute, no state welfare in those days. Mrs Long was left to get on with the little family as best she could. She asked help from no one, independent by will and choice. She turned to her lace pillow to provide the wherewithal for life for herself and the five children.

Honiton Lace in those days was not the expensive and rare luxury it is today. There were women working on their lace pillows outside the cottage doors in Exmouth, in the summer. There were also so called 'factors' who exploited the skill of these humble workers. Often they were paid with half a loaf of bread, or a little supply of tea screwed up in paper. In spite of it all, Mrs Long succeeded and her children came through to make their way in life. In addition to the three Crang boys, their cousin (Mrs Burton's brother) came home shell-shocked, deaf dumb and blind, at a very early age and was compensated with a minuscule war pension. He was able to open a small business, but the effort did not last long, and neither did he.

Let us first take a look at other predecessors. It is stated earlier that Nathaniel is now in retirement, having given way to Tregarthen who took office at the beginning of the Millennium 2000. The Town Council was formed in 1996, having previously been a Committee when the Urban District Council was abandoned. Although as the new Town Council it still remained under the umbrella of the East Devon District Council and hence the Devon County Council. But who were my predecessors? I set up a research into the family tree.

In 1838 a newspaper account tells of the existence of one James Salter, a hornblower. Further research uncovers the following facts: from the time of the laying out of the plantation along the Exmouth seafront in 1838, until the early nineteen hundreds, all the gates of Madeira Walk were locked at nightfall with the ceremony of blowing a horn. This custom is still carried on in Ripon (see elsewhere). James Salter, 1838, was that hornblower! At dawn he opened the gates, one of which was at The Imperial Hotel main entrance (at present), and walked along Bath Road, so called because it passed the Bath House, where hot and cold as well as sea water baths were available. He then ascended the slight rise, now known as Carlton Hill and returned along the cliff and descended to his starting point, having unlocked the gate at the top of the rise. He was in service with others on Lord Rolle's estate. It is recorded that he wore green livery and a silk hat complete with a cockade (a rosette worn in the hat as a badge of office) and as he walked he swung his heavy bunch of keys, which where used at dawn and dusk to lock and unlock the gates, at the same time blowing the horn.

By 1870 Golly, or Jolly, Whiddon was the Town Crier. Whether in uniform with bell or not, I have this on good authority from Ian Cann, Secretary of The Exmouth Society who unearthed a newspaper account of Jolly Whiddon's good deed. One of the things he announced was a reward for a purse that was lost and found belonging to Mr H.C. Adams - The Town Clerk.

In 1917 Harry Whiddon (son of Jolly?) held the office in which he succeeded his father and which died with him. Little else is known, but that which is, is recorded else where in the text.

1985 - The Curator of Exmouth Museum, Tom Haynes, gave me a picture of one Ted Cummings dressed in naval attire, but few details of his life survive.

1996 – Nathaniel Bradley and 2000 - the New Millennium Town Crier Tregarthen Gibson was appointed.

I suspect there has always been a Town Crier, bellman, hornblower, watchman, ever since man started to communicate with man, especially with the advent of state and empires, when rulers of such wished to issue their decrees to the populace of their far-flung domains. There are no clear definitions of the beginnings of town crying. There is very little information regarding the historical background to the office. Today in fact, both ladies and gentleman and couples are involved with the ancient practice of Town Crying. I can only add that today, I, as Town Crier, have a better time than my colleagues from the far distant past. They were punished, sometimes murdered, for non compliance to duty.

I have mentioned previously that the general public concept of the Town Crier is male, associated with the Services in some way, middle aged and often retired. There are others. Professionals, who earn their way by being involved with industry for example. Others make their contribution in the community by opening fêtes and fairs, exhibitions, art galleries, swimming and school events in addition to games activities on sports grounds, and festivals of every kind. Sports clubs, often make demands as do companies, sometimes to open new premises.

My grateful thanks go to Robert Tremain, a fellow Town Crier of Launceston in Cornwall for snippets from his superb *Bells and Yells: the Town Crier's Story*. Further research led me to Delderfield's *Exmouth Yesterday* (1952), whilst other leads often come from idle conversation with colleagues who 'live' in the same bygone days of medieval England, or should that be Britain? (Cornwall being a land of its own). Robert would endorse those sentiments. A fellow by birth as well as pastimes.

The Bible can be quoted, as can the Methodist Hymnal, *Hymns Ancient & Modern,* and a number of other sources. There are many biblical 'texts' from which to illustrate the Crier's art. 2 Samuel, Chapter 18, verses 24-28 for example, or Isaiah Chapter 21 verses 11 and 12. A hymn perfectly illustrates the point, Hymn 16 from the *New English Hymnal*. There are other references for the reader to find and enjoy.

From 396BC onwards, the Olympic Games in Greece were opened by a contest for heralds (Town Criers) and trumpeters. The Olympic Games were opened in Sydney and subsequently in Athens by the heralds. In bygone days, the opening was given to the trumpeter also chosen to give the signal for the various events. The ritual inauguration to choose which herald was to proclaim the judges verdict, was the forerunner of the Town Crier competitions held today.

Stentor was a Greek warrior in the Trojan War whose voice was said to be as powerful as fifty voices of other men. Hence, the word 'stentorian', a word liberally used by Victorian writers to describe bellmen and Town Criers. Today it is still used for contacts between Dawlish and Exmouth across the river! Then – messengers in Greece and Rome ran from town to town crying proclamations and decrees from their rulers to the people in the square. Now – from the Town Hall to the Magnolia Centre in Exmouth.

An extinct civic office today is that of the Mayor's Wait, waiting/watching at the gates and walls of the town, counting the hours of their watch, the time of curfew and occasions of the opening and closing of the gates. Fairy stories and songs emanate from this tradition of which 'Wee Willie Winky, ran through the town' is but one. There are others.

Derived from this office was that of the bellman, the watchman, or latter day Town Crier.

A dear friend, Colin (with glass in hand behind me) celebrating his birthday in the garden, with me as M.C. for the day.

7

TOWN CRIERS THROUGHOUT DEVON AND THE COUNTRY

Pronouncements: Oyez! Oyez! Oyez! Let it be known that this far (and no further?) extends the boundary of the town of Exmouth.

In Pepys Diary, 1660, he makes mention of the Town Crier. 'I staid up until the bellman came by... and cried, 'past one of the clock and cold, frosty windy morning'.

Tuesday 24 July 1870, Falmouth Regatta. The Town Crier a tall grey bearded man in semi uniform and a high hat, stalked in solitary majesty with his bell making proclamation that at 1, 3, 5 and 7 o'clock 'The steam boat, *Pendennis*, would make a tour of the harbour'.

1807, (from Barclay Fox's Journal 1834-1840)come the description of a proclamation of H.M. Queen Victoria made at six points in the town.

We know William Shakespeare knew of Town Criers. In Hamlet's instructions to the travelling players he says 'Speak the speech, I pray you, as I pronounced it to you, trippingly on the tongue: but if you mouth it, as many of your players do, I had as lief the Town Crier spoke my line'.

There is a Town Criers 'Grace', as follows:

O'Lord, who blesseth voice and bell
And helps us when our cries we yell
Please bless this (food, wine, time) that we share
And keep us ever in Thy care.
                    Amen

All cries and proclamations always end:

God save the Queen

For the Cornish only: *God bless the Duke and Duchess of Cornwall*
Everyone: *God bless you all. Peace be with you.*

I received this letter through the Exmouth Town Council office from the lady who kindly wrote to me as follows:

> Dear Sir,
> I was at a meeting where you gave a talk on the work you do and the meaning of a Town Crier.
> You may be interested in the following:
> In Ripon, North Yorkshire at 9 o'clock pm the Hornblower comes into the Market Place. He blows his horn 4 times, says the time and the Mayor comes out of his office. The Hornblower then blows again and says 'All is well'. He is in a dress the same as you. Your talk took me back to when I saw the Hornblower, as it goes back 100's of years. His job in old England was to see the village safe. The gate locked and everyone was in. After telling the Mayor 'All is well' if some one stole in the night the Hornblower paid the fine, as he, the watchman had done his job. So hope you keep that eye of yours on Exmouth.
>
> Thank you for a very good night.
>
> 'All is well', keep up the good work.

It was very kind of Margaret to write to me, I appreciated the letter.

Reference is made to Ezekiel and documentary evidence comes from Ripon.

Oldest civic custom in Britain today is over a thousand years old. The Ripon Hornblower – King Alfred granted charter to Ripon in 886. 'Wakeman' kept watch over the town during the night. He signalled his duty by blowing horn. Today at 9pm the horn is blown by long blasts at each of four corner of obelisk, the fifth blast outside the Mayor's house. The obelisk is 90 feet in height dated 1781. The original horn was replaced in 1690 and itself retired in 1865. The 1986 Hornblower received £1 per day and 50p petrol. No reference as to petrol 5-star or unleaded. Reference is Ezekiel, chapter 33, verses 1-6 and 7-11.

Please note. It might operate in Ripon, but before anyone gets any thoughts about 'What a good idea', I have no ambition or intention of putting the children to bed like Wee Willie Winky (it's past 8 o'clock), or of waking the Mayor prior to starting work! And certainly not paying the fine.

From Ezekiel 33 verses 1-7. The remnant of Israel in the land. These were the words of the Lord to me: Man, I say to your fellow countryman, when I set armies in motion against a land, its people choose one of themselves to be a watchman, when he sees the enemy approaching and blows his trumpet to warn the people, then if anyone does not heed the warning and is overtaken by the enemy, he is responsible for his own fate. He is responsible because, when he heard the alarm he paid no heed to it; if he had heeded it, he would have escaped. But if the watchman does not blow his trumpet or warn the people when he sees the enemy approaching then any man who is killed is caught with all his sins upon him; but I will hold the Watchman answerable for his death.

Whilst researching the relevant sources of information, the Bible played an important part in providing interest in the subject. Accounts of some fierce encounters in the battles fought between conqueror and the inevitable army of refugees. They were left to fight their own battles in poverty, starvation and isolation. 2000 plus marks another milestone in the path of war, this one on terrorism, often repeated in the past, but few lessons learnt of how to combat the scourge in peaceful negotiations of 'jaw jaw' as opposed to 'war war'.

It set me thinking! Suppose the watchman had to report the facts from the watchtower, would he be affected by the news? How would he feel, with a lump in his throat, whilst in the act of giving an account of recent happenings? Compassion? Hatred? Self-preservation? A lonely figure atop a watchtower, the 'enemy' on one side and his own wife, family and friends inside the enclosure on the other.

Thank goodness my duties are carried out in comparatively peaceful circumstances, amongst friendly people and generally it's the good news I have to convey. But what of the different circumstances and how might they be delivered? What of the good news? The interesting events, the happening, the changes. Society that would influence everyone's life and the responsibility resting upon the purveyor of news, the spoken, not the written word.

I am pleased that certain duties, responsibilities of the bygone days do not appear in modern agendas. For example; lamplighters who lit and extinguished gas lamps by use of a long taper and snuffer at dawn and again at dusk. The 'Knocker Up' to herald in the start of the day, with the confirmation of the time and that 'all is well'. The not so good news of the death and consequent funeral arrangements of any member of the community, in order that all could pay their respects to the dead, or more positively to celebrate their lives. The announcement of Births, Marriages as well as Deaths was part of the information contained the pronouncements from national sources as well as local.

The task in those days was much broader and wider ranging than today, which mainly is concerned with publicity of events taking place, locally and the occasional important national news.

I have found from experience that merely quoting from a book of the Bible and adding that the text may be found in verses 1-17 that unless the book is readily available, the identification of the source is forgotten. I have therefore written out the relevant passage concerning the Crier, the Trumpeter, the Hornblower, the Bellringer or the Watchman, all involved with the news they are a sort of human newspaper. Some wider new media is now used to purvey news, views and actions.

But first the list of references in the Bible. These are taken from a Bible passed down through the ages; this particular book is one my grandfather used in the late 19th century.

Not only is the voice heard, but trumpet sounds adds to the cacophony and these historical records reward those in search of facts. Hymns and hymn singing when the theme in the reading needed emphasising were well used. The following are some examples:

In Jeremiah 6 verses 16-20 Exhortations by trumpet-call:
These are the words of the Lord: Stop at the crossroads; look for the ancient footpaths; ask, 'Where is the way that leads to what is good?' Then take that way and you will find rest for yourselves. But they said, 'We will not'. Then I will appoint Watchmen to direct you; But they said 'We will not' Therefore hear, you nations, and take note, all you who witness it, of the plight of this people, listen, O earth, I bring ruin on them to my words and have spurned my instructions.

From the Old Testament - Samuel 2:
Where did it all begin? Who were the Ancestors?

I have spent many sessions with various groups, both locally and throughout the country talking on such subjects as: Trials and Tribulations and yet the Joy of being a Town Crier' or 'The Author Turned Town Crier or vice-versa'. Sometimes, 'A Funny Thing Happened to me on the way to; The Office, The Town Hall, The Village Hall, The Pavilion, The Forum, or wherever the meeting might have been billed. One village I visited had a succession of fliers fixed to the electric/telephone poles stating WANTED. It was only when I read my name attached to the poster that I realised that I was being promoted as performing in the Methodist Hall! I thought it was a pleasant welcome and more was to follow, although it might have been at a later meeting in a different location. However, at the end of my peroration came the epilogue. My references to the Bible in general and to the Old Testament in particular where the Town crier is often labelled 'The Watchman', sometimes 'The Trumpeter', I made reference to specific passages.

But first to the New English Bible. Matthew, chapter 3, verse 1. 'About that time John the Baptist appeared as a preacher in the Judean wilderness' verse 3. 'It is of him that the prophet Isaiah spoke when he said 'A voice crying aloud in the wilderness' and verse 4. 'John's clothing was a rough coat of camel's hair, with a leather belt round his waist, and his food was locusts and wild honey.'

Mark, chapter 1, verse 2. 'In the prophet Isaiah it stands written: Here is my herald whom I send on ahead of you and he will prepare your way. A voice crying aloud in the wilderness, Prepare a way for the Lord; clear a straight path for him' And so it was that John the Baptist appeared in the wilderness proclaiming a baptism in token of repentance, for the forgiveness of sins; and they flocked to him from the whole Judean countryside and the city of Jerusalem and were baptised by him in the River Jordan confessing their sins. Verse 6 John was dressed in a rough coat of camel's hair with a leather belt round his waist and he fed on locusts and wild honey. His proclamation ran: After me...'

John Chapter 1 verse 23 'I am a voice crying aloud in the wilderness...'

Certainly I, personally have no identity with John! My presentation acknowledged in the epilogue, identified me in that of differences. John for example was dressed in a rough coat of camel's hair a leather belt and ate locusts (in full locust bean) a carob, and wild honey. Whereas, I usually am adorned in a fabulous regalia of early 18th century, eat sparingly and although occasionally lose my head, unlike John whose loss was permanent. The mention, however, of 'Herald' has a tangible link, 'the voice of one crying' is another, and at the beginning of a Council or at other meeting, of preparing 'the way' the proclamation is common denominator. It could be argued that there is a remote comparison but little real significance. The main connection is that of Old and New Testament references – a welcome observation that I have incorporated in this text.

From the New English Hymnal Hymn 16 'Watchet auf' contains reference to 'The Watchman':

Wake, 'O'wake! With tidings thrilling
The watchman all the air are filling
Arise Jerusalem, arise
Midnight strikes! No more delaying
The hour has come! We hear them saying
Where are ye all, ye virgins wise?
The bridegroom comes in sight
Raise high your torches bright
Alleluia
The Wedding Song
Swells loud and strong
Go forth and join the festal throng

Sian hears the watchman shouting
Her heart leaps up with joy undoubting.

Neither the New English nor *The Methodist Hymnal* accompanies me when I am met in the Manor Gardens by the bride and bridegroom and the members of both families. Today it is called a 'photo opportunity' and they occur with regularity. The Town Hall is now licensed under new regulations for weddings and the gardens form a splendid backcloth for the photo, especially with the regalia of the Town Crier. So, as of old, The Wedding Song swells loud and strong and all go forth to join the festal throng. Another venue, another celebration another song, to add to the other joys of the Town Crier.

'Tune' Come Ye Thankful People, may be used.

From *The Methodist Hymnal*:

Watchman, tell us of the night
What its signs of promise are
Traveller, O'er yon mountains height
See that glory beaming star
Watchman, does its beauteous ray
ought of hope or joy foretell?
Traveller, yes: it brings the day
Promised day of Israel
            Amen

Watchman, tell us if the night
Higher yet the star ascends

Traveller, blessedness and light
Peace and truth, its course portends
Watchman, will its beams alone
Gild the pot that gave them birth?
Traveller, ages are its own
See, it bursts o'er all the earth!

Watchman, tell us of the night
For the morning seems to dawn
Traveller, darkness takes its flight
Doubt and terror are withdrawn
Watchman let thy wandering cease
Hie thee to thy quiet home!
Traveller, lo, the Prince of Peace
Lo, the Son of God is come.

Hymn 636
Written by John Bowring.
Music, St Georges Windsor, George J Elvey.

Watchman – What of the Night?

From Biblical days to an incident from the Roman legion stationed near Woodbury dated AD96. The account is handed down by word of mouth by one of the Watchmen on duty that night and a message found etched in stone centuries later during excavation of the site.

Cool, but by no means frosty for the temperature, in this part of the Empire is not excessive. It was a cool evening. Due to the celebrations in the camp last night including mead and manoeuvres preceding it there was a quiet atmosphere. Needless to say, the combination of the stillness, the memories and taste of mulled wine accounted for my own inactivity. Indeed it ended with a sulphuric attack of idleness and not being attentive to my duties on this occasion. It had never happened before. The consequences of flogging were then too difficult to contemplate.

What was the incident? Having partially awakened from my somnolent state, I was aware that the silence, in addition to mine, had also overtaken the immediate environment. From my position, high on the parapet, I wasn't at all sure of what? Was it the pounding of feet? Certainly not the feet of one person, but of many. How many? Not only the sound of feet, two or a hundred and two, but they walked nay marched, as one. One moment it was as if they were approaching, the next that they were growing fainter.

44

These noises persisted and grew evermore clear in unison. Then died. And again persisted to disturb the stillness. What could it be? There was no evidence or warning that an enemy was in the vicinity. No legion of the home company was anywhere in the area.

And then, the charge! Not only the feet of the legion. But the feet of the legion's horses. Horses ridden by experts. Years of training and dedication had gone into detail for such a moment as this! All this, the tramp of the soldiers. The horses pounding the ground, anxious to leap out of their harness as athletes out of the blocks at the start of a race. The feeling that, at any moment, something would happen. The foreboding increased in intensity. The air becomes thick with dust and anticipation. Perspiration leapt out of our foreheads. Not only mine. The manes of the horses were damp. The shiny surface of their necks became a receptacle for the excess sweat. The rider clasped their hands together, ringing them as if squeezing the water out that had collected in their palms. No longer were they able to grasp the reins that was the link with their mounts, but the leather thronging slipped, through their fingers, which rendered them useless.

Was this fear? Is this the cold sweat that breaks out and cascades through the very palms, through which up until now had complete control? Was it capitulation to every movement they had been made to perform? But they were so well trained, so well organised, nothing they were told in brigade could change their cold steel like determination than to win!

Theirs was to do and die. They must endure. And so, battle commenced. No more arguments. No further discussion. Nothing left to remember. Do or die. The former was necessary. The latter never experienced. It's Go, Go, Go, Advance!

And so it was. The military machine was about to go into action. Action stations sounded. It was only then, that I, the keeper of the watchtower became aware of what my indolence had caused. Chaos for so many of my friends. I had let them down. I had caused pandemonium. My negligence had been used to turn the tables and allow idleness to overcome duties and responsibilities. And yet, had it? From my position high on the walls of a substantial fortification I could hear the coming and going of horses and men. It grew louder as it vanished. Whatever it was, the sequence had been reversed. Any attempt to advance by the opposition had vanished. The noise of battle about to be launched remained on the slipway of their intervention. They had forsaken the sinking ship, even, before it was launched. No battle scars. No shouting. No noise of any kind.

It was a battle won without arms. Feet which had played an important part in infantry terms were no longer marching. There was no unison, harmony or beat of the synchronised format pattern established after long tedious hours, days and months in training, competitions and practices. All had been forgotten. The horses brought to the apex of their careers as fighting teams were allowed the comfort of cooling down as they moved quietly to the large lake, so often used as their watering place. There, they adopted their single space at the water's edge and ,satisfied, they stretched and turned to their own handler, who with relaxed hands placed them on the neck of their horse to renew the bond that had momentarily escaped both in the hot sticky encounter that never took place.

History in its account of the incident had clarified the story for both horse and rider. Apparently, the invasion force had reported that the fort maintained an unearthly silence, which led the attackers to believe that there was a plot to have them enter the gates and then massacre the invaders.

The simple reason that this or any attempt on the property of others was in the hands of the Watchman. Should he have rung his bell, blown the horn or otherwise signalled 'Let battle commence', there would be an alternative story to tell. Subsequently would be attackers and defenders were united and lived in peace as neighbours.

The Changing Pattern -Not Always What It Seems To Have Been
Quote from Michelle Springs book *Nights in White Satin* – 1999.

I slipped the book from his bag. It was a slim hardback, the faded dust jacket foxed with brown. There was a sketch of an undistinguished looking building and above it, the title: The Spinning House 1635-1894. The author was J. Digby Critchley. He might be an historian as the title page suggested, but I'd never come across his name before'.

'What is it?' I asked. Meaning why this particular book, why for me?
'I found it second hand, going for a snip. There were only ever two hundred copies printed. Thought you might be interested'

'Its about prostitution in Cambridge', John explained. 'No you're mistaken', I said minutes later, after I'd thumbed, enthralled, through the early pages, not prostitution in Cambridge. Not really.

The engraving showed an austere building with rows and rows of tiny windows, The Spinning House. A truly dreadful place. Part workhouse, part gaol.

Dedicated, by 1750, to the punishment of women.

With sixty cells the size of cupboards, I read.
With iron shutters
With no heat, no water, little light, little air.

The Spinning House, where those suspected of lewd conduct were imprisoned.

Where the Town Crier was paid, from time to time, on instructions from the Vice Chancellor, to whip the women and girls.

Having lived in Cambridge ever since my own undergraduate days, and I've never before heard of this place. Ancient Universities like tradition but only as long as it makes them look good. Powerful institutes don't relish reports about their less savoury pasts.

At home on another birthday; just the two of us in the glow of early evening. Forget the clock - essential for all Town Criers!

8

FROM UNIVERSITY TO TOWN CRIER
– ANOTHER CHANGE –

Altogether, I spent 42 years in Education, retiring in 1985. If ever anyone does retire. Now with my wife and 3 grandchildren, 2 of who have partners, a daughter who lives nearby and the son who prefers Roehampton to Exmouth, I am spending more time with them and with Marjorie. We were married in Stratford-upon-Avon. She is still the long-suffering, delightful and understanding wife with patience personified. Having spent most of my life with other people's children, it's a great joy to be with one's own and I love it, and them.

Now in the autumn of my life (don't they come around ever so quickly? That's a reference to autumn!), I had finished my book *Exmouth, Her Age Of Elegance* and given up my responsibilities at Dolforgan Court, where we live now, as a former Director of the Management Company. That was four or five years ago. I had lived with a timetable all my life. It was my intention of not doing so again! Intentions are not always fulfilled. I have, today, an

Louisa Terrace, Exmouth, and Dolforgan Court (left) with bay windows and turret.

extended diary, already pencilled in for 2005/06. I had to busy myself with a new activity. I wished to be involved and contribute to a wider community. You will remember how it came about, by being bullied, cajoled, as I have written, and was asked to be the Millennium Town Crier. After all I was slotted into the substantial workings of the Town Hall as a volunteer, unpaid, ecumenical, independent, apolitical, but wishing in the new era to help in putting Exmouth firmly on the map as the largest town in the county of Devonshire, with all its attributes. 'Sometimes you don't choose your career, it chooses you.' I much enjoy my present position simply because I like meeting people.

But, I knew nothing about Town Crying! The answer? Find out! I didn't think I would be involved with writing about it. I wanted to do 'something about shouting'. I began researching wherever, whenever. This meant attending one of the competitions held throughout Devon and neighbouring counties, even further afield in counties far beyond the South West. The Town Clerk and the staff saw to it that my term of office as the Millennium Town Crier and Member of the Ancient and Honourable Guild of Town Criers began appropriately in 2000. Why? In retirement? I was issued with a diary and finally returned to the timetable!

All thoughts of maintenance of Dolforgan Court had to be put on hold - including the gardening!

9

EXMOUTH EXPECTS

Flying the flag, Exmouth, Excellent, Exceptional, Enterprising, Excellence, Exemplary, Exquisite, Extol, Exciting, Expectant, Encouraging, Endless, Evolving, Executive, Earnest, Exuberant, Exact, Execute. Each containing a message that could be run up the mast of Exmouth.

Linked as it is with the sea, sailors and all that have their being and livelihood in going down to the sea, the signal run up by Nelson prior to the famous victory sounds as good a chapter heading as any other, and better than most in the situation. In the historical writings authors usually begin at the beginning. Any attempt to do so in the case of the history of Town Criers would have quite a search as the start seems lost in antiquity. There appears to be no beginning in the sense that a line is drawn to mark the start of the custom. Little is known or even passed on by word of mouth regarding the start, although it is more than likely the tradition was handed down from generation to generation, from father to son (although in the 20th century certainly the 21st, it could be expressed as mother to daughter). This implies that there are lady Town Criers. Yes there are. And what's more generally better looking, better dressed, and their presentation is often a winning one in competitions. In fact there is a husband and wife team who have the responsibility of organising one of the Guilds of which some Town Criers are members.

My personal choice or perhaps the first one that came into my orbit was the Ancient and Honourable Guild of Town Criers, founded some 25 years ago. It has the usual structure of Officers including an Editor of a Quarterly Magazine, suitably named *The Crier*, in addition to elected members of the Committee. The President is drawn from the membership, usually retired, but has maintained his stance as an elder, overseeing his large family. At times, usually when competitions are organised he is in charge to see that the rules, laws and general standards of dress are maintained. Presentation and many other facets of life facing the competitor are satisfied under the experienced eye of someone who has himself had that unique moment of judgement. A further section spells this out in more detail.

However if I am to adhere to my original outline plan, I should at this stage perhaps head the section, How I Became a Town Crier. But before I do, maybe a little more background is necessary to put this particular person in the group of existing cryers in this country. Now isn't that interesting? As I write, pen in hand, I have written 'Cryer'. I have often asked why do we, at the beginning of our cry shout Oyez!? And why cry? And what do we call a collection of Town Criers, a bellow? A quire? Talking newspapers? Messengers? Watchman? Bellmen? All will be revealed. I have heard all this before and still not a collective noun to cover us! Family of Town Cryers?

I was asked recently to write a personal account of what might have been subtitled 'adventures of a Town Crier in the new Millennium 2001.' I know little about the art/science/foolhardiness that enabled groups (usually) of men, often in middle years of life to don regalia, robes, buckled shoes and tricorn hats. Then to take up a focal point in the centre of the town and shout their heads off. The picture I have drawn has far too many discordant colours, and it is not only for the men!

The average age of a group, bellow, gathering, shout (whatever the collective noun of a member of Town Criers maybe) is reduced considerably by the ladies who tend to be younger, certainly prettier in themselves than the males, who are peacock like. In fact resident in the north of the country, a married couple form the team in the town. Never mind the team in the town, the competition in the kitchen must be warm, if not hot! Their house might be named 'Decibels'. Well, I am always out and about and the observation is often made. 'I don't know that I would want to dress up like that.' The kitchen requires clothing appropriate for the function, place and time, so does the Crier!

Many of my now colleagues have followed this edict and have a number of uniforms to suit the occasion. Some of them are true to the middle ages if that is an historical date time, and that's nothing to do with the age group or the size of their waists. The regalia is designed around that period of time. The office was of course to assist people who could not read relying on the interpretation of the stained glass in church windows, to absorb facts, which otherwise they would not have seen. And here was another opportunity to not only to see but hear the word. Dressed in colourful regalia and ringing a bell was the early edition of the talking newspapers. How interesting that it is now common practice to have talking newspapers for the visually impaired. Records, tape recorders, recently DVDs replacing Town Criers? Lets hope not! For it is the tradition that enfolds and captures the format of what is said, who says it and how they should attract their fellows. Bells and cries.

I begin my research! Memory is a prominent feature in everyday life. The absence of it, particularly when elderly, is sometimes embarrassing. I'm told on reflection that it is only recall that is missing. We retain much but recall little, especially when it is needed. I have, therefore, spent sometime exercising my recall, usually comfortably ensconced in a large armchair with cushions admiring the view from the bay window. I sleep! No recall! But after sustained effort and motivated by 'deadlines' and talking, talking and talking, a glimmer appears. I rapidly write it down. And here it is! 'A Day in the Life of A Town Crier' – I remembered. It would take me a few years to repeat previous performance but it comes within the compass of the itinerary and I have had the experience.

Why?

In setting the scene of why I became a Town crier, I have to refer to the book *Exmouth: Her Age of Elegance* which I completed in 2003. I endeavoured in that treatise to place Exmouth in its rightful position in Devon as the oldest seaside resort and the largest town in the county outside the conurbation of Torbay and the cities of Plymouth and Exeter. It is today, the Western Gateway Town to the World Heritage site on the Devon and Dorset coast.

When I was asked to be the Town Crier of Exmouth and enter into the medieval world of costume and culture, little did I think that it would throw me into the world of historic research, the world I had been long linked with in researching the previous book on Exmouth. However, when challenged that's exactly what one has to do – devote the time necessary for this activity and interest. First and foremost, I knew little about a Town Crier. I do remember once as a small boy hearing the 'Oyez! Oyez!' shouted with an accent that could only have been uttered by a Cornishman, 'Ahar ahar' wafting on the breeze in either Town or Market Square. Had it been echoed anywhere else the cry would have met with the usual southwesterly gale, dominant as it raced across the Plain-an-Quarra the predominant feature of this noteworthy town in West Penwith.

However, the message was loud and clear. The bellow when absorbed by the many citizens who heard it, including me, emanating from this decorated elder who was informing everyone. 'The water be cut off from 11 o'clock of the hour 'til 5 tonight. B'aint be no more watter 'til Wensday. Us hav bin waitin for 'un to be on tap, for thirty years, ad 'un for 'bout 5 minutes, now is off'. A rough translation but without the Cornish accent!

This meant for me and many others that we had to revert to the 'stand barrow'. This piece of equipment was essential for those who did not have water, supplied through the tap. It meant for me another trip maybe two, to the village pump with the stand barrow. Wheeled as with a normal wheelbarrow the major difference was that the specialist construction had a barrel which was so balanced across the sides that it was capable of being tipped fore and aft. Well experienced in this exercise, I visited the pump in Lafrowda Terrace filled the barrel to half its maximum and wheeled it home to Mum. She had a washhouse in the back garden.

In connection with the Town Crier, I recall on the Annual Feast Day the meeting of the hunt in Market Square. He was present, not dressed in the red jacket, riding boots and astride a horse with dogs running around him. No, he was standing alone without the stirrup cup in his hands but a yard of ale, which he swallowed with a flourish to clear his throat for the full cry. Not a sound from the hounds or the horses. The Town Crier's clear bell-like voice, echoed from all sides of the square. 'Cheers to 'ee and good comfort to all gathered together on this our Feast Day.' The closing statement of 'God Save The King' sent horses and hounds in pursuit of the fox. The King was remembered. The hunt now almost only a memory. The Queen remains.

A similar account, I'm not sure from where it came refers to the Crier 'dressed overall, but on Feast day he always returned'. He 'opened' the Feast with a draught of ale. A welcome to all and his other engagement apart from visiting the remaining inns was at the Meeting of the Hunt in the Town Square. The poorer followers sped on cycles or ran or walked to the vantage points around the surrounding country encircling the town, to 'follow' the hounds.

To complete this circle of duties. The Town Crier always returned whenever the 'watter be turn'd on again' and life would revert to its quiet pace with coloured water from granite tin and copper mine workings for the few moments from the time of the 'switch on'. The only other 'switch on' in the home was the Aladdin Lamp, powered by oil and wick and then homework to finish. Who was this strange figure of a man? Dressed in 18th century costume, shouting to a mesmerised population that there was no more water. Confused and frustrated by this intrusion into what had been a miracle, 'running water' someone demanded further information. Drawing himself up to his full height and taking a deep breath which seemed to come from his rather full cushioned midriff, he replied or rather continued his proclamation concerning 'The Water Supply'. In short, he reminded us of our long wait to have the supply connected, 30 years was mentioned. Now another lengthy drought was forecast. 'No' he said 'I can't tell 'ee how long is givin to be for the turn on. Try again dreckly'. When translated dreckly, could mean, well anything, probably not that which was similar in the precise pronunciation of directly.

In reality having waited for the first connection, time was of little consequence. Accuracy was not required. Minutes, hours, days, even months was of no importance. In fact, did he not say, earlier in his pronouncement that 3o year's gestation was not out of the ordinary? So much for what he said. Actually, it does him an injustice for he then drew on his formidable supply of oxygen and with a burst from powerful lungs announced it brighter lighter tones, 'Now for the good news' The Carnival, but 'ere' he said, 'afore that' someone somewhere had lost a purse, should it be yours you were asked to collect said container from the office in the Church Hall. No indication of colour, size or content was forthcoming. All would be revealed in the necessary inquisition in the Office! Even more excitement, awaits those who had not lost a purse!

In even more excitable tones of joviality the forthcoming Carnival was to 'proceed in an orderly manner throughout the streets of the town, through the Market and Bank Squares and Fore Street on its way to the sea shore' it was quite clear that everyone had to take part, floats were already in preparation from last years journey. Groups, families, sporting associations, church and chapel, institutions of whatever colour creed or derivation, including schools were instructed to attend. 'Its some 'andsome to see they tots dressed up and walking and waving to their family' was the encouragement accompanied by several bouts of bell ringing from our visitor.

But not for long, did the mood last. A smile removed from his face by the back of his hand, admittedly with the assistance of lace cuffs worn by this eccentric character, was replaced with the downbeat look of someone about to change the mood of those watching this performance. It was to be more serious in content.

This was made quite obvious when, with the now clearly observed intake of breath. 'Yu will be sorry to 'ear that old Charlie died last night' The news was received with a period of silence. Those not familiar with the town and its population had no idea who Charlie was or might have been and now wasn't. 'Ee died well he ad'nt been well with the missus 'olding' is and'. Everyone now knew. Charlie had died not forgotten and the additional fact and information that the missus was there, so he was not alone. The provider of news had completed 'his contract' so had Charlie. But the connection was not lost for the final statement from the obituary as pronounced by our friend was heard, 'I went to school with he, am as old as 'ee is, or was, and it do make 'ee think!'

Such is the pattern of life, a constant unending circle. Many of Charlie's friends and perhaps work mates would join together at the wake when announced and walk solemnly through the town, taking often the same route as the carnival, but the bell would have a quiet muffled ring. The ring would be pronounced when all were together to give joyous thanks for Charlie's life. This ceremony follows another format, invariably handed down by father to son and has not changed over the centuries. Often the coffin is borne by the bearers many of whom are friends of the deceased and always at shoulder height. The procession is led by a large photograph of Charles carried by the strongest friend. Followed by the Town Crier with bell ringing at suitable intervals to summon the occupants from within to come out of their homes to join in the joyful praise for the departed. This mini group is completed with selected music makers who accompany the growing group with traditional tunes. All reminiscent of Charlie, much to the obvious enjoyment of the family who in their various ways are giving thanks for a life, knowing that he would have appreciated the thanksgiving. The entire company, having walked the main street return along the same route and in the Church or Chapel Hall, hear poems read friends, eulogy given by, none other, than the Town Crier and the family also pay their tributes to Charles.

The final scene, sometime after private cremation, is enacted on the bridge over the little stream, which flows through the gutters of the street recently walked. On the green banks the final act to the accompaniment of the music and formal farewells, the ashes are scattered. So begins yet another story and yet another diary entry in the life of a Town Crier. No other births, marriages and only Charlie's death is recorded today.

* * *

However, water is still in plentiful supply, certainly at the beginning of the 21st century, the first 100 days of rain were sufficient although still expensive throughout the west country. The future of the hunt will be determined before the rain stops. But change there has been and will continue for better, for worse, for richer, for poorer, often until death us do part. One thing is true the Town Crier is involved in most of these everyday happenings. The result? I had to continue to research Town Criers and in the process to look at documents over the years, including those of the Ancient and Honourable Guild of Town Criers.

Summer fun at Exmouth, 2005. Look for the Alpenhorn.

The modern summer Carnival Fun Day each year in Exmouth spans over two consecutive weekends, the emphasis is on 'Fun'. Disco dancing for the young on the Green. Inside the promenade music supplied by an intricate array of wires leading to the speaker loud in output but nevertheless necessary for the dancing activities. The not so young having put baby to bed, supervised by nana had encouraged their teenagers to enjoy themselves. Out in the twilight, made brighter with the array of lights along the seafront all joined in the fun. There were no Victorian Waltz's, or strip the willow, not even a barn dance, certainly not progressive but while there is music, people will dance and they do! Energetic, inspirational every muscle exercised the gyrating dancers engaged in informal ever-decreasing concentric circles, until fatigue catches up with the 40-50 plus group who made for the beach to 'cool off'.

The dancing continues. The music blares. There is always one of these Fun Days to ensure that the remainder of the fair comes to town. Whirls, shakes, fast and faster go the mechanical machines. Round and round and round again. Carrying everyone higher, wider than self propulsion ever achieved, although in descending to their loved ones awaiting their return, they often leave their stomach behind! Enjoyment? Certainly! But there is always the sublime quiet roundabout or the choice of the horse you can ride. The accompanying music is powered by the huge golden organ. It explodes. Expires. Draws breath from its mechanical bellows, and then attempts another half hour of supplying wind to ensure that the insatiable appetite of the horses galloping up and down in unison is satisfied. They look almost effortless in their complicated controlled movement. Meanwhile there is the food and drink area. What a good idea!

Food for the fellow. Food for the lady. All can be had at the stall. There under the exhausting heat of the hotplate, everything is possible. If it's cool, you want? Try the ice cream parlour. Ice cream parlour! Well the cart wheeled into the arena to cool the customer. There was plenty of both. Customers with cornets, customers in long queues, customers in delighted groups and demolishing multi combined creams, a sort of instinctive con-glomeration of the celebrated knickerbockerglory. Fantastic and fun! And that's what it's all about and now cooled; slowed down, back to the music and the promenade with the invitation still sounding loud and clear from the untiring music maker. He's great!

Whenever one is faced with a decision, it is often the case that pause for thought is uppermost in one's mind. But the sudden death of a colleague brings one abruptly to the loss of a friend and the significance he or she has made to the general public and in the community. They have served, usu-ally as a figurehead or focal point in their immediate environment. For years they have probably led the carnival striding proudly out in front of other outrageously dressed citizens, walking or, marching closely followed by the strikingly costumed Town Band. That figure in front is the Town Crier.

He, or maybe she, engages, massed crowds in 2, 3, 4, or often 5 deep columns along the processional path. Shouts of glee, shouts of pleasure, an occasion-al pause in the pace whilst the rear of the caterpillar endeavours not to lose the head as it winds its way through streets decked with bunting and the static column will burst into song, celebrating someone's birthday! Who? It matters not. It must, after all, be someone's day of birth. Children often sit-ting on the kerbstone, watched carefully by mum and dad, or maybe by nanny or grandpa, who from the relative comfort of the wheelchair, watch over their offspring with pleasure as they all join in the chorus of 'Happy Birthday to You.'

Some folks have the added advantage of the balcony view from the upstairs window, perhaps a front bay, and from their aerial vista drop their pennies or the pounds into the blanket carried by a well-trained team of sea scouts who from each corner of the collecting material, gather up the coins that have missed the centre of the mobile bank as it, too, winds its way along the prescribed route. They receive congratulatory thanks for the contributions and are encouraged by the bell ringing Town Crier to float down some bank notes, which will add to the reward of the proceedings. It is thought that first floor followers of the Carnival are more prosperous than those children sitting quite comfortably in the gutter. Health and Safety never far away in community gatherings and throwing of coins is now forbidden. Nothing could be further away from any thought of 'darkness' There is an over-whelming air of praise, passion and thanksgiving. The sounds are magnificent. The bandsman, puffed with enthusiastic blowing, red-cheeked and with contorted facial expression gives the impression of ultimate explosion. It is explosive. The sound that emits from such exaggerated contortions is translated into harmonic rapture with their colleagues as they march in regal fashion along the well-trodden path of their fathers and maybe grandfathers who were once boys in the band.

Today we can now add girls in the band. But these are not the only noises crackling through the air. The regular pattern of feet striking the ground, the timing of the slow march. But hush! Listen! Is that the swirl of a kilt I heard? The air is disturbed. It must be the swish of material barely covering knees. The air is being contained! In a bag under one arm. Both hands are encouraging fingers to stop the air escaping though the pipes. Yes! It is! A favourite pipe band with magnificent best dress always worn on these occasions. But it is the regular bang; bang of the drum that now sets the pace. The big drum! Usually the biggest drummer. He stands erect, balancing his big drum on his big belly and bang! bang! bang, bang, bang! Gives the skin of the circular container, literally being beaten by a big, big, bigger drummer who has a heavy weapon with which to beat the drum, it seems unmercifully. But it has a profound effect upon the waiting population. They cheer! They clap their hands! The children leap out of the comfortable gutters in which they have been residing and shout, clap and if there were room, dance to the tune of pipe and drum.

And suddenly, as they came, so they go. The sound fades gradually. But it has left a warm glowing feeling, a sense of a job well done and it allows the spectators an opportunity to see the next item in this kaleidoscope of sight and sound. Time to look at individuals. Those who have sufficient 'get up and go' to enter in the parade. And what have we here? The clown, juggling clubs, using his skills in keeping 3 or is it 5 tennis balls in the air at the same time. The old-fashioned pram, full of big bouncing babies. The fairy princess with flashing lights throughout her fairy costume. The sea scouts in their attempt to slow down their run away gun carriage. The endless number of children in their fancy dress. The lights, the noise, the heat generated by thousands of electric light bulbs on long trailers decked with scenes from the past, present and even into the future. These 'floats' controlled by the inter-com with skill and dexterity edge these huge beasts on multiple wheels around the town hardly designed to accommodate such monsters with the greatest of ease, whilst the dancers danced the fugitives fought, the music blasted and bounced on a generation of caterpillar type vehicles which raised the question 'when would it ever end?' But end it did.

And with the end, a succession of vans, cars marked clearly with red crosses for those in need, colour-coded police cars for protection, and cleaners who virtually cleaned through the night for that which had been discarded, the rubbish. A footsore Town Crier linked up with those of the same calling and enthused crowds wandered home talking frequently about the order of merit for individual attempts to compete for the prizes.

A memorable day for all the participants. This is October and the Summer Carnival is the main operation which funds the Illuminated Winter Carnival. The former is more of a funfair which by virtue of voluntary activ-ity by a group of dedicated people who arrange a fair, close the promenade and the fun begins. The money raised at this function is to a large extent used as a float for the main event later in the year. That's another kind of 'float', which is essential for any Carnival!

'Float' an odd word to use in Carnival time. At one time there used to be a Water Procession of boats and ships dressed overall held on a balmy evening in fading light. On return to 'the buoys and girls' they left behind on the outward journey along the sea front, they returned with port, starboard lights and additional coloured lights to add to the Carnival ambiance. A splendid sight. A Water Summer Carnival. What a splendid thought. A thought translated into action. First, gather together those that go down to the sea. Voluntary bodies, sailors, boatmen and women. Giggs (both sexes now involved), yachts, cats, rowing boats of every shape, size and condition. Propelled by wind. Magic kites controlling surf jumpers, the possibilities are endless. And then there are those who look after all at sea. The inshore lifeboat crew, helpers and supporters, volunteers, voluntary are middle names to each and everyone. To add to the sea faring and sea fearing fami-ly are the Forward Team of Birmingham. No not another midland football team, but a gallant formidable crew manning the Exmouth Lifeboat in over-all command by the Skipper or Coxswain who excels at gallantry and is cer-tainly formidable. They in prime position could lead the flotilla of sea going, estuary explorers and beach boys and girls afloat whilst the followers followed on aboard the Pride of Exmouth and add a touch of class to the whole parade of water borne activities afloat. How about it? Something for the future? Next year?

A bright summer's day dawns. Except for the mist, but there's much warmth present. Not only the warmth in the greeting of those who pass by with that cheery 'Aren't we lucky to live here?' but the atmosphere that's in the air. As the minutes tick by, so the air becomes warmer. Somewhere, actually it is in the East, the sun is no more than an extinguished halo, done its best, yesterday, and now wakening to do rather better today, but still sleepy and surrounded by cotton wool like heat maze. The circular ball radiating the kind of heat those cauldrons of metal daily pour out of blast furnaces. It will require such a temperature to demolish the fog, which has now formed into banks of white foam like cloud. It will also require many more confirmations of the luck we have to live on the coast, exposed to see mist. But the day dawns. Soon everyone can feel the heat. Another day ahead!

The Town Crier's lot is a happy one, unlike the policeman in the Gilbert and Sullivan Opera. There is of course an exception and that is today. Temperature has a profound effect and affect on the conditions in which we work and play. I have already made reference to the blast furnace, and added to that sphere of employment would be the chefs, the kitchen staff and those who work in extreme heat. Taxi drivers even must while parked be conscious of the warmth generated by idling engines eager to get underway. not only to earn their living but in need of air, cool at that, flowing through the cab window. There are many other occupations similarly affected. These people in the course of duty have by virtue of their office to wear a uniform, not only as a mark of identification but it is usually restrictive and devoid of acclimatisation from freezing to unbearable heat. The uniformed populace are hard done by and maybe Gilbert, or was it Sullivan?, had drawn an accurate picture.

This particular crier has two sets of regalia. One used as a working outfit and another kept for civic functions. The first in green medieval in period was adjudged by general public as not worthy of the exulted position. When questioned many accused the wearer as faded or fading and reacting to the questioners grimace, quickly replied that it was the green cloth that was fading and on no account could they accuse the Crier of losing his colour! The second outfit, really to avoid the intense sunlight generated in the South West generally, and Exmouth in particular, had to be confined to indoor ceremonies. There are many of these from talks to a number of groups and societies to the opening of shops, fairs and fêtes. Visits to many exhibitions, the Museum, schools and colleges, churches and chapels, homes and gardens and countless voluntary bodies. How is it managed? It is first a case of pacing oneself, walking on the sunny side of the street and when climatically its too warm, in the shadow of the appropriate side of the road. Always walk or stroll!

Walk, walking another topic worthy of consideration and worthy of mention. Communication, which is the ultimate objective of the Town Crier. This is best done, when not enclosed in a carriage of any sort. Certainly it is more difficult and can in that situation reach only a few people who share the travelling vehicle with you. So its walk and walking, fitness is necessary. Practice essential. And what better means of communication can there be than walking with who ever? Speed is controlled by the slowest, which seems sensible. A group of walkers can choose their company. Walk out with one person, home with another. Share conversation with your partner(s). Both are engrossed in their own company and if the group meets regularly, the sessions are eagerly awaited. Choice of route is theirs. No fear of contamination from the fumes of the cars, lorries or buses. The system employed in East Devon and other areas reaches a peak in Exmouth. Named nationally 'Walk This Way', it is a scheme (Tuesday and Saturday mornings from Manor Gardens in Exmouth), initially set up for those who take little or no exercise. Just what the Doctor ordered for the Town Crier.

There are now three groups. Those who wish to satisfy the original conditions. A number who wish to move on and up and not stay on the level, but can manage an incline, and finally, in this part of the world, those who now have moved to Grade 3, and will go a little further and faster in the allotted time of approximately 1.5 hours. A special group whose first steps were with Walk This Way now undertake an agreed time and excursion into the far beyond, but all return to the focal point for the welcome cuppa or light refreshment to regale each and everyone with their exploits on that particular day. It is very much 'a large family outing', with a genial atmosphere. Sharing is a useful and necessary activity.

Another special group enjoys sharing, sharing in the history of Exmouth. Along with a number of towns, no doubt, there are some interesting fascinating dwellings in our town They are designated as buildings of some importance architecturally and historically by a blue plaque. A trail has been established for residents and visitors alike who together explore by walking. They have been most successful and in both areas of endeavour, our thanks to those responsible for staffing and encouraging all to take part.

Those of us who live in Exmouth are indeed very fortunate. We have passing through the town the 632-mile walk around the coastline from Minehead, Somerset to Weymouth, Dorset. The coastal path. When it reaches Orcombe point, Exmouth, the walker is faced with the Western Gateway to the Jurassic Coastline, another 95 miles (155 km), but a walk through 185 million years in front of them. It is established as the Natural Wonder of the World. It only remains for you to take out the boots from the box in the attic, don some old favourite clothes and set out on an adventure in the world, starting here in Exmouth.

For those who cannot, there is always the sea adjacent to the coast and using that facility there are other adventures beginning here in the slipways for you to try, including a cruise along the Heritage Coast.

Walks of another kind? Motivated by the quite superb gardens in Exmouth and the yearly competition, Britain in Bloom, there is in addition to the Blue Plaque a ramble through the floral delights of the Town. This is arranged by the enthusiastic team of Exmouth in Bloom. A delightful experience and one for Spring and Summer. Do not miss, however, the storms which bend the palm trees on the esplanade. The sand dunes diminish in height. The roads become strips of sand radiating from the salt sea spray which has mounted the old sea wall and come into the town.

This combined with the remarkable sunsets all the year round makes Exmouth the ideal focal point for nature and nature study. The river abounds with its flocks of wild winged foreigners who visit once every year, and they become fond friends when they return each year to exactly the same spot to nest. Welcome is written in many ways for many. All are welcome. And so shouts the Town Crier, daily sometimes, as he walks along the seashore

Walking is an occupational hazard to some but essential to the Crier.

Summary of Trails
Mention of Trails must include, in addition to Walk This Way, The Blue Plaque and extended walks from Exmouth. The *Explorer* publication is illustrated by the trail through gardens, parks to see the most delightful varieties of trees, shrubs, plants and wildflowers. These walks are listed in a colurful pamphlet replete with remarkable pictures of the walks. Second only to Taunton in Britain in Bloom, Exmouth is renowned for its parks and the outstanding work carried out by the staff helped and assisted by a young, (well younger!), Tidy Group. Congratulations to all responsible for and involved in winning the trophy Britain in Bloom 2005. Magnificent!

But having been on 'A long walk' or several of varied lengths, its time to come home. Home sweet home. The situation may change in different areas of the country. I came across this article in the *Manchester Evening News* of Tuesday 9 July 1996 (this is not misplaced, it was filed under 'The Crying Game' - author):

Unlike most couples David and Julie Mitchell like nothing better than a good shouting match. But their yells are not directed at each other. The first time Julie's husband made her cry was arguably the best career change he ever made. For Julie was eventually to follow in the footsteps of his fancy buckled shoes and join him in the crying game. Together they act as a civic voice for Vale Royal and the city of Lancaster. It all began with a peal of bells on their wedding day. They had planned an historical theme for the occasion. Unknown to Julie, David had also arranged for the Town Crier of Chester to awaken her with a proclamation. Due to unforeseen circumstances this was not possible. David pleaded and borrowed spare livery and a bell and himself brought tears to the eyes of his bride to be. 'Arise, fair maiden, cast off thy slumbers and clad thyself in fair refinement' These days, Julie prefers to start the day 'more gently' but David's surprise gift inspired their future together. Together, the couple will issue a personalised message for those celebrating a special occasion. In every day terms its called sharing, not only in their relationship with each other but also in sharing with others. They are not unique. There are other married couples involved with the art of crying, but historical facts will give them a first.

Julie admits that the public appreciation of her husband in his crying role influenced her own 'calling'. She joined him first as an escort and then as a Town Crier in her own right. She says, 'It was a leap of faith. You don't know what is going to happen next, but once you've got over the initial shock its exhilarating. One minute you're working with a Knight or millionaire and the next entertaining at Aunt Ethel's 70th birthday party. What you do makes a person's day and you know they'll talk about it for ages, which thrills my heart and brings a lump to my throat.'

Julie is proud of the equality she and a number of other ladies share with the country's 190 male criers. There maybe a few more ladies recently joining the ranks. However, Julie's last comment is typically female, 'Its rather odd having to tell your husband to straighten his tights and fix his wig'. They, the ladies, will always have the last word! I personally am grateful to Julie and David for sharing their bonding-together with all the readers and individually for another facet of Crying. Thank you both for your contributions.

David has been connected with, and member of as well as an officer in the Loyal Company of Town Criers for many years. The couple concentrate on the historical significance of the events they are proclaiming. After dinner speaking, appearances on TV but basically they still adhere to the bell and the voice to communicate with a number of people, proposals, nuptial proclamations which are among events that occupy their skill and expertise in performance. In the kitchen, they have significant silences. David tactfully sums up, 'we are professional Town Criers so don't shout for nothing. If we do fall out, Julie with a deafening call, quells further disagreement by shouting 'Tea's ready.'

Some of the influences and motivation involved in the act of Town Crying include detailed instructions. Flow in the Footsteps of 'his' fancy buckled shoes. Don the brocade waistcoat and tricorn hat of the 18th century. The peal of bells on the wedding day. The bell inviting one to school. The land bell signalling silence whilst one joined one's class in full and handsome livery. The epitome of Georgian Gentility. A Gentleman. Handwritten on parchment scroll the name of the Town Crier who is of suitable character,

A cutting from the Exmouth Journal, January 2004, reporting on the award of Citzen of the Year. The author receives his award from George Maddaford, President of the Rotary Club.

The author as seen by his granddaughter, aged 5

THE ANNUAL TOWN CRIERS COMPETITION
IN NEIGHBOURING TOPSHAM

Right: Doffing my tricorn at the end of my Proclamation of my home town, Exmouth. I declare 'God Save the Queen,' and the company reply 'The Queen!'.

Below top: left to right - Rosalind of Hatherleigh, the author (Best Dressed award), and the host, Jon of Topsham.

Below centre: The assembled company singing 'Land of Hope and Glory' conducted by David of Gloucestershire.

Bottom: Spectators gather to see the assembled Town Criers at Topsham. Seated in front row are some from Exmouth.

Above: A photo-opportunity at Dartmouth. Competitors are given 'Bells Up!' and the sound of the bells is accompanied by the choral singing of the Criers.

The author in his new regalia made by Sara Radford of Exmouth.

Below: At the annual fete of the friends of Exmouth Hospital.

Left: The World Rugby Cup comes to Exmouth.

Above: Exmouth's Coat of Arms

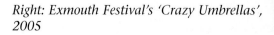

Above: A decorated Wessex Train coach is welcomed to Exmouth

Right: Exmouth Festival's 'Crazy Umbrellas', 2005

Above: The author in Holy Trinity Church, Exmouth

Top right: Competing at Dartmouth

Top centre: Proclamation at All Saints Church, Exmouth

Right: Shortly before being 'kidnapped' in aid of Children In Need

The author in Exmouth

The Millennium Town Crier of Exmouth, an oil painting at the Magnolia Centre by Vicky Holloway.

A studio photographic portrait of the author arranged by Kay Foster. Note the Honiton lace jabot, early badges (c.2000), gloves, bell and scroll.

Outside the Pavilion on the Esplanade waiting to greet those attending the Mayor's Charity Ball, always held on the seafront, usually on the last Saturday in May.

punctual, courteous, articulate and above all reliable. A sedan chair for the elderly useful with elegant uniformed footman. It may be necessary to have voice training, exercises for the diaphragm, the difficulties of throat infections, coughing is detrimental when in mid flow and disastrous if continued, medication, usually in liquid form is the popular remedy, but alcohol is questionable, menthol and eucalyptus in hot water has been found satisfactory if inhaled. Hecklers are to be avoided but shouted down at all costs. Drinks are obviously to be given a wide berth; the ultimate put down in front of an enraptured audience is definitely the cure. A personalised message for those celebrating a special occasion is most welcome. The public appearance of the Consort/Escort gives added pleasure to both Crier and Escort/Consort. As a result of this and other aspects of the fun the terms' conviviality', 'ambassador' are usually heaped upon the successful. What, who is successful? Make sure your tights are straight and fix the wig!

Having a captive audience is often a hazard. One has to ensure that they are being informed and entertained. The latter sometimes overtakes the former and the good Crier will use this opportunity to underline the informative. Questions are raised in competitions as to whether gestures and body language in particular should form part of the presentation? The other end of the swingometer is formality. Poise, grace, discipline are other characteristics are floated, discussed with vigour and give a wide range of presentation.

What? Is a question left undecided? Ambassador is the answer!

10

ANECDOTES, INCIDENTS AND HAPPENINGS

The Millennium Mayor, Councillor Ron Mudge recounting in his memories and highlights of his year in office recalls: I was due to meet the young children from 'Chernobyl' who were visiting the council offices. I came, on this occasion in my usual attire, but thought it might be an interesting exercise to ask the children to help dress me as the Mayor of Exmouth. They were delighted and I remember their enthusiasm when handling the jabot, the lace and robes as they attired me in the Mayor's Regalia. A moment to remember, for me as well as the children. Unfortunately, the Town Crier was away in London at the time, but I did borrow his bell. The children enjoyed seeing the polished article well known throughout Exmouth and were delightful and delighted when each and every one of them rang the bell. Reporting the visit of the children, the Mayor listed this event as most memorable. He drew much pleasure from the contact with the children, as well as delight that Exmouth could offer comfort, kindliness, and compassion. All could derive much knowledge and appreciation of the lot of people less fortunate than us in this country. Literally, a moving incident with a bell, which provided great joy in having the opportunity with the Mayor to ring the Town criers bell.

I did, during a 'follow up' visit meet one of the youngsters and he too remembers the incident. In fact he rang the bell again! He was accompanied by his mother, who was able to thank all concerned in her own language, Russian,'Spacebo' (phonetic spelling). An interesting exchange.

Several other sessions of groups visiting Exmouth who were invited or often wished to attend 'Local Government begins here'. A tour of the town hall, followed by further interesting facts together with questions asked of the Mayor, if in attendance or whoever happened to be attending the meeting. There are many foreign language sessions over a few days in Exmouth and these young people are welcome from France, Italy, Germany, not only Europe but as already has been described, from Russia and Eastern Countries.

The whole sequence of Twinning relates to the office of the Town Crier.

The five mayors of Exmouth since the Exmouth Council was formed in 1996. They are Councillors Geoff Chamberlain, Trevor Cope, Ron Mudge, Pat Grahame and Brenda Taylor. The photograph was taken at the Mayor's Annual Charity Ball, 2004, at which the author was M.C.

The author and Mayor, Councillor Pat Grahame in Langerwehe, Germany, which is twinned with Exmouth. Here they are seen visiting, and particpating in, a demonstration of pottery-making.

Exmouth is twinned with Langerwehe in Germany and with Dinan in France. Neither of these towns have the office or appointment. The robes and regalia were a new experience for the Twin towns. I have been a member of the Association for over twenty years, not in one span, but spasmodically as the situation changed and as priorities change during that length of time. Only two Mayors have had close links over that period, although there is a Civic Reception for whichever town visits Exmouth, that is every year when the Mayor and dignitaries have the opportunity of meeting French and German Representatives from their country.

Another society/Association/Group of people who through their voluntary work create an atmosphere of friendliness and fellowship. Yet another team that earns and deserves our admiration for that which they do for others.

There are so many examples of this outreach. Recently on a visit to Exmouth were a group of people from Wick. Not twinning, although not beyond the bounds of forming an association. After all it is Scotland! They came to celebrate the close link many of them had with H.M.S. *Exmouth* in the Great War. The ship was sunk in Scapa flow with the loss of 188 hands. It was a sombre occasion but one that contains sorrow and yet joy, the former for the 188 souls, the latter for the obvious pleasure, fortitude and comradeship of all who served in the ship. Many were gathered together for the first time, the second generation having the opportunity to thank their predecessor for the courage they had showed in the darkness days and deepest waters.

It was a celebration and again thanks to all who made it possible.

A celebration in different circumstances and different venue: I was invited by my hostess in Langerwehe to take part in a play that was being staged in one of the surrounding villages. I was delighted that other members of Exmouth were included. Some of the remainder attended the fête, part of which was this sensational play. I never did find the author, but then I could not understand the German anyway. It was too quickly spoken, but, however, an Action Play! It was much enjoyed by the large German audience. The medieval costumes were 'made up' the evening before in a combination of the Adult Centre for continuing education and Leisure Centre. Both aspects were covered in the entertainment. I'm not quite sure, but do remember that it was a pageant play, a sort of *Canterbury Tales*. My companions and I were peasant travellers caught up in this cavalcade. The farmyard was alive with animals being fed and watered. The company with one rehearsal, acted superbly.

The scene was set, the village 'en fête' and the players arrive. The dance, the songs, the movement all took place on a stage in the centre of the farm dwellings in the yard, a sort of theatre, and produced a most significant spectacle for the play which was based on a pilgrimage and the pilgrims appeared in procession amid to the delight of the assembled throng of villagers. The animals were involved and played an important part in the evening. The music came from the players, as well as songs and the theatrical verse.

The combination of the language the interpretation of some of the traditional dances to say nothing of the music all meant one method of following the curve of learning. Rehearsals proved valuable! A grand day for pilgrims.

Remember? The first lady Mayor of Exmouth was Councillor, Mrs Brenda Taylor was in her second year in that Office, before I was appointed as Town Crier. She however was largely responsible for my elevations! Nothing compared to the heights Brenda achieved. She was poised on top of the tower of the Church at Withycombe. 'Now abseil down' they said. And she did! 'Follow that' was the cry, I looked up the insurance cover and decided, that's not for Town Criers! Brenda has now been elected to the high office of Deputy Chairman of Devon County Council 2005-2007.

Following Brenda's term of office, she was asked to talk to various groups of her life as the First Lady of Exmouth and sometimes I accompanied her on these visits. I came a very poor second as the volunteer after being cajoled into office and accompanying the Mayor to a number of events. However, they were most enjoyable and good fun. The number of voluntary groups in Exmouth who held meetings to which we were invited were many and varied. All seemed to enjoy our contribution. It took the form of a brief historical background, the regalia, the contribution everyone made to the traditional structure of the office, together with the more formal council meeting seemed to be of interest.

At Christmas time, I remember, the cards we received usually hand-crafted by clever participants of one of our local groups were the topic of the afternoon. However, as part of the celebration of Yuletide, Exmouth has a Christmas Day swim from the beach in front of the clock tower to the lifeboat suitably made available as a safety boat. Hope was 'at hand'. The lifeboat was moored, conveniently and ominously offshore together with other safety water-bound craft. Imagine the scene. Some 250 in the water, four times, often more than that number watching from the shoreline

Visiting Santa's Grotto at Christmas. I'm not sure who's visiting who!

beach. The countdown before 11am begins! Ten... nine... The Christmas card reads 'It is the long established custom in Exmouth that the Town Crier at precisely 2 minutes to eleven advances clothed in the regalia of the Town and at the hour appointed rings the bell then plunges into the water in full uniform to surface as near the lifeboat as possible. We the townspeople of Exmouth look forward to your total immersion and subsequent resurrection from the deep.'

Three... two... one... Go! That's when I dived for the insurance policy again. What group had I joined? What had I entered into? Abseiling clock towers, entering freezing water, if not with ice, the air would be seasonably cold! Bitter. And furthermore this was my future. The Christmas card is fact. I awoke from my dream and although the whole experience was concerned with water, I was bathed in perspiration in my endeavour to reach the lifeboat.

With the former Mayor, our second lady in that office, Councillor Mrs Pat Graham when we were both faced in the Council Chamber by a group of some young people from Italy. They were on a study tour to learn English and have a look at local government. The Mayor, as an elected representative, the first citizen, the tasks was comparatively simple. At least that's the skill of the Mayor who was able to draw the thumbnail sketches for those who do not necessarily understand the language. Given the added advantage that she had finished her tasks she then turned to mine. 'This funny man will tell you why he is dressed as he is and what he does'. Ringing the bell is a good start and on asking my audience 'and who do you think I am?' I progressed from pirate to admiral in one session of half an hour. Such is fame! Such is promotion.

Back to research, leads me into a text I once talked about to a group 'you will only find success before work in the dictionary' Something to think on! Well, who would have thought, I certainly didn't that in the new millennium in 2000 that I should 'be dressed overall' wearing a tricorn hat, a jabot, lace cuffs, white stockings, buckled shoes, pantaloons, patterned waistcoat, frock coat, collar festooned in embroidered badges ringed with a badge of office around my neck and wearing white gloves. It was said 'he's nearly an octogenarian gone 79 anyway'. Now, I am writing my personal autumnal days as a Town Crier in Exmouth, or in the context of this document writing about interesting experiences.

My youngest granddaughter, then only 6, one day held my hand and took me into my bedroom and crept quietly to the wardrobe door. She peeped

Pirates? No just four town criers in full regalia. Here we are seen at Topsham and it would appear that Jon, the host, is endeavouring to help the 'Old Man' in a 'Senior Moment', whilst Nick of Bodmin and Robert of Colchester obviously enjoy the situation.

through the crack of the partially closed door. 'I think there's someone in there!' She opened the crack a few inches more and standing, clutching and pulling me with her saying 'Yes, he's still there' She pointed quite clearly to the partially opened door and with her index finger as if to convince me; 'There, look there!' Wondering who it might be, a moth? A bee? A butterfly? Who or what might have been hiding in my wardrobe? I asked 'who is it'? Have you seen him before?' 'Yes, yes' she replied and added the additional information in an excitable voice, 'It's a Pirate, grandpa, can't you see him?' Without waiting for a reply she further clarified the situation. 'He's been there since breakfast'.

It was, of course my regalia, hanging from under a shelf which was accommodating my tricorn hat, followed by the cape, the coat and on the floor of that section of the cupboard, the buckled shoes and white gloves with much lace in evidence. I had not regaled my family that my new Town Criers outfit had arrived.

As a result of this mistaken identity, I now own a parrot (manufactured) which can perch on my shoulder fastened down, a black patch to cover one of my eyes and I am working on a lathe to produce a suitable wooden peg leg, at the same time practicing my 'Aaarh lads, its doubloons I'm after, before the excise men arrive. Hey Ho! Follow me! Aaarh me hearties! Shiver me timbers.'

But there are compensations I do have photo opportunities, 22 in one day, not taken with soccer or the cricket teams but by visitors on whom the Town relies economically. It is not that aspect of my life which is the more difficult door. The one-labelled Welcome is open and with a friendly smile the conversation seems to flow. That in itself is a clear indication that leads to a return visit to the town. Special occasions are remembered.

More Incidents and Happenings
It is plainly evident that having been involved in the life and work of a number of people, knowing them little or not at all, that they should, due to the practices of burials, cremations or internment, all be brought together in one or other of these ceremonies. We may have had a unique experience of this ceremony.

Imagine, for example, four black horses, dressed overall in their black plumage, festooned by shiny brass buckles, a picture indeed from a county show, horse trials, or from our exhibition of carriages used on ceremonial occasions. The carriage itself, a visual delight. Polished to perfection. Glass glistening. Tracery in the glass, golden throughout. The whole framed in the hearse with a platform for two attendants, who themselves, appeared to be competition with the pure colours of the cortége. The shaft surrounding the horses gleamed. The belt, buckles and bells on the two sometimes four, triumphant animals added power to the delightful picture.

The entourage arrived. Outside in the street, the neighbours looked hesitantly, not wishing to be directly involved but not wishing to miss a fleeting moment of the arrival of Tommy. Up until then he had been in an unfamiliar place for him. Now he, Tommy, followed by aunts and uncles, nanny but not grandpa who had a similar farewell a few weeks ago and the contest was on as to who had the best dismissal! Then the team of assistants met up with the team captain in his top hat, and in a thoroughly splendid fashion slid the coffin into this beautiful glass hearse. The silver band, previously hidden in a neighbour's garden, stepped out and stood, before moving off, with bowed heads.

At a simple signal of a tap on the side drum, they really stepped off at a full stride of 36 inches in true military style. We were on our way. Those following the hearse in their own time bearing no military flags or pomp and circumstance, in fact, 'in broken time', trailed their way through the streets.

These were packed to capacity. Children sat on the pavement, with feet just over the gutters onto the road. They too wished to be near Tommy. They waved almost apologetically as he, in all his glory, rode by. He would have loved this honour being paid to him by so many, especially having requested before his death that the procession should be led by the Town Crier in full regalia.

In another world, who knows? In this world in the 21st century, it is certainly that some provision, perhaps not quite so elaborate will of necessity be arranged, if not by us before the event, then by the loving families. The one certainty in life is that arrangement has to be made in advance. It always reminds me of Carnival time. Giving thanks for the life of one who we love and admire and giving thanks that it was our good fortune to have known the person who contributed so much to our life.

Incidents in historical records are open to criticism; handed down through the ancestral chain and depending much on the winning team, usually the teller. But there are a few tales that did take place. These were not those that relied upon accuracy but merely the ability to tell a tale sometimes from make-believe information. But a third comes to mind. It actually happened to me! Actually happened, no make-up, no cover up.

These incidents are usually due to bad luck, forgetfulness, paying little real attention to detail. Acting as a Town Crier is usually played out in front of an audience. Some 5, 10, 15, maybe more, people. Situations arise where 100 could be added to each of the examples given as a starter. But no matter how large or small the community, congregation or audiences that stand in front of the Crier, they are expectant. They thirst after information. They wish to hear in loud tones the message to be delivered. Often they say 'We've seen you in your Robes, in the town' which deserves the reply 'Never mind seeing me have you heard me?' The people who gather to hear have to be satisfied, if not one soon loses the high regard that yesterdays shout gave you on the clapometer!

Innumerable numbers of the public, usually from abroad, that not only includes that majestic country divided from us with the Tamar, but also from further north, west or east. Apart from the normal chatter and exchange, such as 'where are you from', or a comment on the climatic condition of the day, there soon follows the request quote 'Could I have a photo of you with Aunt Elsie.' Another photo opportunity passes and friendly exchanges are made and invitations exchanged 'Come and see us again.' Followed by 'You must come to Newcastle upon Tyne' or 'West Midlands' and in the mean-

Please may we have our photos taken with you? Summer visitors from Germany with the author on Exmouth beach.

time I'll show them your photograph with me (and Aunt Elsie). Elsie might of course come from further afield in the antipodes.

Communication, meeting people, welcoming them to their immediate environment, making their stay in our town even more comfortable by a friendly gesture and a welcoming smile. There is much to be done in a large town, which is now approaching 35,000 people. Relationships are important in life.

Many places, and Exmouth is no exception, have registered offices where marriage ceremonies are held. The Town Hall is one such place and one of our most beautiful parks, Manor Gardens, surrounds the Council offices on three sides. Needless to say these well kept, delightful creations of mans control over nature (or is it vice versa?), whichever affords newly weds their superb backcloth for their wedding photographs. It also happens to be on the route followed by the Town Crier who is then involved in a special welcome to Exmouth, in addition to the longevity call of 'May you both have many happy years together.'

11

COMPETITION

I have elsewhere in this story of town crying that there are some very funny incidents. Many of these occur during and many more after 'The Town Criers Competition'. The event is heralded by flying banners, often commemorating a feast day or some historic event that requires an annual event. The Criers assembled are usually asked to meet in the Town Hall, and might include 20 or so members chosen for their allegiance to their National Body or Guild of Town Criers. The Mayor is in attendance. He or she might eagerly anticipate a day in the sun listening to shouts of Criers from individual members invited to attend. But before the 'fun' starts, the structure of the day has to be broadcast. And although the bell is the beginning of any pronouncement, it is the gavel that calls everyone in the Council Chamber to order. This ancient custom is the responsibility of the ' Home Crier', who understands the procedures, after sometimes, 30 or more years service to the community. How many Mayors have they had to invite to say a few words

Exmouth Carnival 2003. Left to right: Steve (Dawlish), Geordie (Cullompton), Steve's escort Caroline, Phil (Warminster), and Roy from Ilfracombe.

to the assembled company? Never mind how many. This is another year! The first citizen of this year then thanks all for responding to the invitation. A careful warning has no doubt been issued. 'Not too long Mr Mayor, Madame Mayor'. Always bearing in mind that the communicator of the day is the Home Crier, and he/she usually has something to say about the making of history this year. He/she has no other function than to introduce distinguished guests, ensure the rest of the day passes without major hold up, that food and drink are provided and every detail already discussed is available for all attending.

Having listened attentively to the Mayor, he then invites the overseer of the competition, often a retired respected member of the Ancient and Honourable Guild, to ask the Mayor 'to make the draw'. It is a custom to ensure that the Criers will perform in the order agreed by the draw. This is somewhat important, for a number of reasons. As the day progresses some of these will be revealed but tend to be more serious than funny; 20 to 30 is perhaps the average attendance, sometimes more, as in the case in 2003 when 127 Criers attended the World Championships in Newquay, Cornwall. But I am out of order! The draw, well it does make a difference as to whether there are 20 or 120.

Competitions are usually held from 10.30am to 5.30pm with a suitable break for lunch, having had a good breakfast and looking forward to the evening meal. A change from challenge and contest into one of friendship and fellowship. Not that I have encountered any confrontation, but it is a contest. The draw has been made, the resulting order is on the printer and everyone knows after whom, and before whom they appear. Off to the arena! Well, what can it be called? The open-air entertainment area? Maybe a bandstand in the middle of town, sometimes a well designed performance stage is an elegant park, sometimes a milk crate on a balcony looking down on the assembly below or podium, a strongbox, like surmounting stairs and thank goodness a rail to assist the climb and finally to curtail any falling off the box. Such is the diversity. Experience is the grateful asset of those who face the hazards repeated, perhaps once a year. The pattern is moulded to suit the needs and maintained wherever Town Crier Competitions are held.

The Home Crier now performs. He/She (Criers are from both sexes) will usually introduces himself to the congregation, no, spectators or listeners, maybe, and follows this by giving a few lines of what is termed in the profession 'a benchmark.' Presumably this is an effort to accustom the listeners to the way the wind blows. What is the atmospheric effect of the environment, and to set some sort of standard. Many of these experienced Criers do just that, but it is the standard that can be daunting to those who follow. And here they come in the order in which they were legally drawn with no favouritism, no distinction as to large/small/coloured/pink/Roman Catholic/ C of E, all with one purpose to entertain, and receive the approval of their endeavours to inform and educate and shape the community activity of the day.

Rules and regulations are laid down before application or invitation to attend the competition and these are usually strictly followed. Any variation would mean loss of points for 'the cry'. The day is divided into 2 sessions with a lunch break in between, morning and afternoon. Those who have reached the senior age grade have to be particularly careful. Food can be soporific and to doze after lunch would be catastrophic. The host Crier did invite everyone to enjoy themselves, eat, drink and be merry, but he has the advantage of being unable in anyway to compete as his duties as host means his time is taken up by oiling the wheels of this visiting caravan of fun and ensuring that timing is of the utmost importance.

A succession of 'Oyez!' called three times in varying tonal quality, decibels measuring the strength. The strength necessary to ring some of the bells that individual Criers carry, can by the end of the day, sap any surplus energy required for the performance. Depending on the terrain and positioning of the podium, four or five judges are carefully sited to have every detail recorded.

THE PITFALLS OF THE COMPETITION

First, the waiting until the call to the rostrum, nervous moments take over, and surrounded by the public, some of them, staunch supporters, but colleagues who before were companions, now become not compatriots, but contestants. No longer are they the kindly friendly partner and member of the Ancient Guild of Town Criers but they become the antagonist, the opposition, the ones to beat and leave having thoughts that they had chosen the wrong activity for their retirement. The nerve endings are uppermost. Thoughts flow and become a torrent of the competitive stream. Where once flowed slowly, babbling through the sunlit bank side, now a raging disturbed fluorescent leaping wall of water cascading down and down taking all with it in its undisputed path. Meanwhile the next contestant tries to shake off the nervous temperature that has suddenly descended, but finds the shake too much of a trial. Nevertheless the show must go on and in an endeavour to ensure that he is not the one to give in first, straightens his jabot, then tips the tricorn hat to tilt at an absurd angle, having first adjusted the deco-

Prizewinners all at Topsham. Clockwise from top left: Paul (the winner) and host Jonathan; Robert of Colchester, Nick of Bodmin, and Geordie of Cullompton.

ration of flowers or regimented badge which adds colour dignity and identification to the wearer.

Your name is called. Now the entrance. Upright stance. Smart walk. Good bearing. Servicemen will be easily recognisable by the thumbs which will be uppermost lying that on a clenched fist. When unoccupied the said thumbs will finish in line with the seams of the trousers. When in action they will complete the movement at the end of a straight arm, shoulder high, having kept the thumb uppermost supported by the clenched fist. The whole movement is effortless, toes pointing in the forwards direction, head up, eyes front and endeavour to take in any steps, rising several feet high with ease and confidence.

Having arrived at the 'delivery point' panic sets in! Where is the shout? The one which was altered when dissatisfaction set in. Where was it? Having agonised what seems to be a quarter of an hour, while the crowds wait, fingers tremble as they grasp the newly found script, and ensuring that it is the correct position to read, start with a BANG! Not that sort of bang but a clear shout, emphasising the final consonant clearly with authority and clarity.

The Oyez!, Oyez!, Oyez!, the opening clarion call is made to everyone, hoping that they will be listening to you for the rest of the pronouncement. A flutter, sometimes prolonged, often enthusiastic clapping, announces to everyone that having heard 'God Save the Queen' the shout is finished.

The return of the other contestants is the reverse of the opening. One tries not to show self-confidence in the walk. Equally so not to be in despair, holding the eyes of the judges and audience. In any case, there is little to be done, the invitation to perform, the performance itself, is finished. It might not have been one's best, but it's now for the judge's decision.

During the tenth Town Crier Championship of the World and the 25th anniversary of the Ancient and Honourable Guild of Town Criers (of which I am a member) held from 10-17 May to inclusive in Newquay, Cornwall, the skills itemised were as follows:

Volume and clarity, diction and inflection, discipline and best dressed. The content and accuracy of any cry is always checked by the competition co-ordinator. Judges are usually spread, North, South, East and West, sometimes enclosed in a marquee to prevent them being influenced by gyrations or unnecessary movements of the Town Crier. Marks are given for the performance in each of the sections.

The Mayor of Exmouth, Councillor Mrs Eileen Wragg, accompanied by a body-guard of Town Criers during the Exmouth Illuminated Carnival in 2005.

The World Championships attracted a number of Town Criers from many parts of the world, including UK, Australia, Canada, Belgium, USA, Netherlands, Holland, Poland and would you believe it, Wales is even listed, and since the competition was held in Cornwall, no doubt there was a Cornishman present, if not two or three!

I wrote the following letter to the Editor of *The Cryer* in 2000, the year I was appointed, and four years later I have put together the observations made in that time. There are many supporters on both sides of the argument.

Dear Sir,
Thank you for maintaining contact with me as I set forth on my journey of exploration into the land of Town Criers!
   I did take the opportunity of visiting a number of towns in the West Country and as a member of the public to attend some of the competitions in the festive season of carnivals.
   I have subsequently received the latest copy of The Crier, *and the notification that I was appointed Town Crier of Exmouth at the Mayor making ceremony in May 2000 I did make a few notes on my observations which may be of interest, and happened to be relevant to comments made by the magazine and other Criers.*

WINNING CRY: Exmouth town crier Garth Gibson

GARTH HAS PLENTY TO SHOUT ABOUT

A press cutting reporting on a civic occasion which demanded the author wear full regalia: the lace jabot depicting Exmouth's magnolia emblem and clock-tower.

I must admit to inexperience and obviously that I feel comfortable at various times and in various situations. For example, the atmosphere at Remembrance Day Ceremony is different than when faced with hundreds of children involved with 21st birthday greetings for Pudsey Bear for Children in Need. The shout for the Christmas lights will be in complete contrast to the ceremony of the induction of the Mayor, him or herself, or of the new rector of the parish church. True, place and circumstance must be the guide.

So too, must the content of the cry. There are necessary skills to be perfected. From the audiences we face comments made include repetition in more formal cries, much of 'sameness' varied organisation and presentation of event, the topic of second cry too formalised, which, when summarised is identical to the Chairman's thanks for those who write and air their views which I have tabulated for future reference.

My opinion would be toward a freedom of presentation, with competition regulated and points scored, but the second cry when the choice of content would reflect the personality of the Crier is all his/her splendour to match their colourful regalia.

Greetings from Exmouth

MARKET RESEARCH

Ask a broad audience:
> What they think?
> What aspects are enjoyable?
> What more or less of what?

The content of one's cry informs and educates and when well written it can entertain.

Competitions: Arguments follow two directly opposed views: Old v New? Ancient v Modern? Formal v Informal? 20th v 21st century?

Deadwood	New Growth
3 Oyez! from erect position	More drama on the podium
Start point, eyes front, one Escort	Hand gestures, with smiles and frowns.
Restricted to mould, centuries old	Greater creativity and imagination
Flowing continuous cries	Original and entertaining
Formal home town, marked out of 100	Informal cry, anything goes, 50 total
Old friendships renewed	New friendships to make
Meet others of the same ilk	Do what we do and enjoy it as we do
Contest, rules and regulations	More freedom
The past tied to tradition from Centuries long bygone	The future? The best of the past combined with the present
Uniform approach	Freedom of Expression
Technical, technique	Artistic and entertainment
For ourselves	For the audience
Aged and genteel crowd	Dynamism
Obvious supporters	Showmanship
Pomp and circumstance	Free expression of delivery

Uniformed automatons	Informal movement
No character or individuality	Frustration
Formal- Listen to me	Striking up a rapport
Bore audience to death	Swagger confidently- entertain
Dressing like Peacocks	Individual gestures
Sobriety in all aspects	Humour and laughter
Speak like newscaster	Life contact
Voice is dominant	Acting Skills
Received pronunciation	Body Language
Controlled practices phrases	Long pauses
Stand still on podium	Delivering an art form
Routine- unchanging approach	Ability to mesmerise
Read from the scroll	Very visual interest.
Emphasis on accuracy of text	Do what we do and enjoy it as we do it
No hand gestures, smiles and frowns	Capture a wider audience
Precedents have been set –do not vary	Ability to do one's own things
Collective clones	Local accents and talent per- formance
Tightly bound	Free to move
Structured	Flourish in competition
Hard and fast rules	Familiarity and individuality
Humourless	Encourage audience participation
Rules constrain	Memory-not read
Part of our Heritage	Modern approach
Introverted	Being oneself
Remain motionless during cry	Flexibility, is important

Playing it safe	Creativity and imagination
Colourful regalia – Ring the Bell	Extroverted
Winning, Prize and Prestige	More for fun and satisfaction
Dignity all important	Unusual and innovative
Loud authoratitive voice	Change in tone and emphasis
Stentorian, dimensions and decibel	Engaging the audience
Madame Tussauds dummies	Anything goes. Swing of pendulum
Prestige and traditional	Drama on the podium
Approach, ignoring all others	Entertaining the audience
Conform, Conform, Conform	Perform, Perform, Perform

The judges have a framework to which the criers adhere including stentorian dimensions in decibel. In addition consideration is given to clarity, inflection, pitch and difficulty is an added quality. Usually there is a minimum of 75 words and a maximum of 100 including 3 Oyez!'s and 4 stated giving allegiance to the Queen.

At the AGM in 2004 some rules changes were made in the respect of future competition. The main one is in respect of the 'cry'. There are now only 4 categories! Volume, clarity, diction and inflection. Discipline has now been removed after marks have been monitored throughout the past year. Best dressed is an entirely separate category and the marks must not be incorporated with those awarded for the cry in any circumstances.

The joy of giving the audience the pleasure of seeing, hearing and enjoying the spectacle during competitions is I think reward for the competitors, and whether they agree or disagree with the judges is entirely subjective, and the decision is theirs and theirs alone. May it long continue in that spirit.

Who is to say? Who is to define? Who is to judge? Which rules? Who? The public in our region of cry? The locals to whom the cry is made? They give out the vibes of the popular? Entertaining? Enjoyable? Change the rules hometown cry followed by fun cry. Does it have to be stereotyped and serious or free choice of subject with free expression of delivery.

I am indebted to Michael Wood, Crier to the East Riding of Yorkshire, for the bones, the skeleton of the right/left side, the black and white, the old and new, negative and positive. It is for everyone to adorn the skeleton in whatever structure form they wish and to enjoy the creation knowing that it is controversial and may stir the blood! So much for Adam, then there is Eve, to be or not to be.

Another memory bank stored in the Town Crier's Pandora's Box follows: I have been introduced to a number of voluntary activities, both as a visitor and often as participant. I am amazed at the number of such groups. The dedication to those who organise is remarkable. The members of those groups whose work, skill, expertise together with the positive action that they take to establish such high standards, almost entirely for the benefit of others, often less fortunate than themselves. They are and remain an inspiration to everyone. Exmouth is blessed – there is no room for boredom!

During 2000 and 2001 I visited and was involved with 84 such organisations. The following year my visits to organisations had risen to 158. In the second term of office, with the second Lady Mayor, the total rose to 231. Last year compared with the present year it fell by four to 227. This year to 1 November it is just over 100, but by the end of the civic year, which isn't until the Mayor Making in May 2005, 365 days in this year, 366 in the leap year 2004 would suggest a visit everyday. Not quite accurate in fact, because there maybe as many as 3 per day often with evening appointments. There is still much to do, even then, there are many people in this largest town in Devon outside the 2 cities of Plymouth and Exeter and the conurbation of Torbay. The population of Exmouth now exceeds 34,000.

I have also been fortunate in working with the team within the Town Hall. Successive Mayors have been extremely kind and helpful. The Town Clerk John Wokersien and his team are always ready to do all that is necessary, answer any questions, and to make life that much easier in a friendly atmosphere.

Anyone asked to make a career as Town Crier might be considered suspect about his or her future. Many are recruited during the retired period of their professional life. Sometime this is an added qualification in having seen a little of the world and been involved with people at work and play. Military men formed the background of the corps, or what might be the collective noun for a group of Town Criers a Bellow? Ringers? Bellmen? Criers? Shouters? The historical background of what they do is lost in the mist of antiquity.

Above left: Checking the Proclamation before delivery to a family audience in the Rose Garden, Exmouth. Right: A photo-opportunity with a vistor from Italy and a colleague, John, from Truro.

There is a school of thought, which gives credence to the large staff or pole or thin rod being carried by some officers. It is thought that the Crier is also the Mayor's officer, a sort of bodyguard for the town's civic leader. Some carry the staff. One crier states 'there have been two incidents where I have had to use it, once when a gentleman of middle eastern origin tried to get hold of the Mayors chain'. He later explained that in his country 'if you touch the person of power then that power was partly rubbed off on to your self'.

I have many enjoyable moments. None more than so than when I meet people. But if I'm not a pirate except in dreams and in the vivid imaginations of children then I must be a Town Crier. Older children, admittedly from overseas, thought that I might be a sailor and after 30 minutes or so I was promoted to Admiral of the Fleet. Although most of us through childhood, school stories, and vivid imaginations are surrounded, bombarded by life's rich pattern and emerge as something quite different. Research and then living the life, I now know more about Town Criers than I did 4 years ago. Not many have that opportunity or want it! Fly away from it! To avoid his/her in this summary I have kept to the more common 'he'. It is not clear who is he? Clearer, who appoints him? What qualities are necessary for the occupation, varied? How long does he stay in office? Until death do us part in some cases? And why is he dressed in that funny, well, unusual garb? Tradition? Further more, not only he but she as well. Yes, there are a number of ladies who are also Town Criers. Some of the questions have been answered. Some will remain unanswered. I have no doubt there would be many different answers to some of the questions.

What is the Court Leet?

John Sweetman, Town Crier of Truro, Grampound with Creed is to be thanked for this interesting article which first appeared in The Spring 2005 edition of *The Crier*. Thank you John.

In mediaeval times communities were not administered as they are today, by local and regional governments. But each lord of a manor was authorised by Royal Charter to administer his own estate. This was done by the establishment of Courts Leet and Courts Baron. Courts Leet were courts of minor criminal law, which had the additional major function of appointing and empowering manorial officials; whilst Courts Baron were courts of customary or local law. This system existed throughout many centuries and it is only over the last two hundred years or so that changes have occurred, culminating in the present day process.

The Alcester Court Leet whose records indicate that it was probably first constituted in the year 1272, has, unlike the vast majority of other courts, continued functioning from that time without a break, albeit with ever decreasing hours, and has gradually become what we have today, a tradition orientated organisation, which amongst many other functions, upholds and maintains the colour, pageantry, and ceremony from times gone by and which are now so much a vital part of the Alcester scene.

Sufficient to say that there are nearly 200 Town Criers in this country and here is one who had a few difficulties! A neighbour in Town Crying terms was left stunned when a fresh faced community policeman approached him in the street and told the Crier to keep the noise down! My only experience involves two young ladies support officers in the police force, who have arrested me twice, in fun, much to the anguish of on lookers. No further action was taken.

But I have been arrested, marched off, secured in a stockade, a queen's ransom paid to release the Exmouth Town Crier after he was kidnapped. It was reported in the local newspaper that 'fearless Garth is just terrified, taken out life insurance, plotting an escape to the Far East.' The kidnapping was part of the University College rag week to raise money for Children In Need.

Students from Rolle College, Exmouth, kidnap the author in order to raise money for Children in Need. £1760 was raised for his release.

Another charity helped. I usually class these incidents as the trials and tribulations of Town Crier and yet the joy comes from the smiles emanating from the people one meets. A further joy and pleasure from those who derive the benefit, usually less well off in many ways than most of us. A joy it is forever, well perhaps not forever.

By and large I do have many enjoyable, moments. Sometime ago I was invited to the celebrations arranged by a local primary school. They were celebrating 125 years of continuous education on that site. The children, under the guidance of an energetic, interested staff, had worked hard to mark a very special occasion. There were many parents, families, and members of council and county dignitaries. I was dressed overall, in a number one uniform, and chatting to a group of people. I was approached by a young boy. He must have been 6, maybe, and when I congratulated him on his sixth birthday he wanted to know from where the information came that he was 6. I further quizzed him asking whether he in his class was the only one who had lost his teeth. Mesmerised he said he didn't know! He said that I had asked him a question could he ask me one. I agreed. He stepped forward, tugged on my frock coat, and said, 'ere' as they do in this part of the country, 'ere, is it true that you was the first 'ead teacher of this 'ere school?' Childlike, honest, inquisitive, no conception of the span in years that I needed to cover, but it inspired our group to laugh with one accord.

Schools, because they contain these vibrant, inquisitive youngsters are a source of mirth truth and realism. Visits to the museum is a sure method of raising their curiosity and the questions are fired automatically or in quick firing bursts. In the recreated front room of a terraced house upstairs in the museum was a dummy Victorian lady dressed in a suitable overall for the task she was about to complete. She was standing at a mangle. I thought I might help her, at least to wind the handle to rotate the rollers. There were some sheets in a wicker basket, which she had obviously finished. Clean and pressed. I stood by her, and she might well have asked me, that if I was going to help, I might have changed my clothes, instead of wearing my regalia. However my duties did not permit me to do so, and I continued in my efforts to assist a lady in distress.

I heard a noise of feet coming along the corridor. A group. A family per-haps. And they appeared. My eye moved. It was the only part of me that did. I stood quite still hardly daring to breath. My partner in work had no such difficulty. Being stuffed and having no breath to draw she remained motionless. My breath, however, came and went quickly! I recognised my 6 year old from my recent visit to his primary school. He brought or was at least with his sister, two brothers, mum and dad, and I am sure it must be have been Nanny. He approached me. Ignoring my workmate who remained stationary, he circled around me and having completed the joined up circle, produced the index finger of his right hand. Without warning he placed this rigid finger quickly and strongly into my solar plexus. I doubled up attempted to catch my breath but it escaped. Meanwhile, my primary friend triumphantly exclaimed to his entire family 'there, I told 'ee 'e was real' and added, 'I met 'im in my school on Tuesday.

Here are some more, any of these could be expanded into a serial story. Children in jubilee celebrations in street parties with food and drink and dressing up. Presents of mugs available at community parties and genera-tion celebrations. Visiting children at peace in hospital. Active children. The 250 on the beach at jubilee celebrations, the sand sculptures, the play readings, the music centre, the clowns, the story teller, sea shells on the sea shore, parachute practices on the green, all on one day, with a picnic lunch and ending with tired children.

Another day to remember would be the 11th hour, 11th day on the 11th month at the war memorial when young children lay a wreath on behalf of their relatives, perhaps grandpas who had lost their lives, a poignant moment for the sister remembered by the child on Poppy Day at the war memorial. There are so many memories, school assemblies, visits by dis-

Top left: The Mayor, Councillor Pat Graham, laying a wreath from the Town on Remembrance Day. Top right: A moment of silence at the War Memorial. Below: At Widecombe-in-the-Moor in 2004, with the President of the Rotary Club and his wife, at the annual outing for Cream Teas with the elderly of Exmouth.

abled children to theme parks often by taxis or loaded into private cars and the delight that the children had given to their escorts. Not only children. What about cream teas in Widecombe-in-the-Moor for the not so young? Wonderful! The festival holds unforgettable scenes with children on the move, the singing, the play acting, the decorations made from painting, drawings and art work on exhibition for all to see, and collectively being altogether contributing to a massive kaleidoscope of colour, movement, and active participation for the benefit of others. It is amazing! One last observation, whilst playing my duel or multi-role I was accosted by a small boy who said 'you've just missed father Christmas 'he was here, five minutes ago'. Just a matter for me changing in to red costume at the appropriate time of the year.

Maybe, just another comment on the Town Crier by the Town Crier. I am often asked 'how long have you been a Town Crier'. I usually, depending upon the audience, answer 79 years, followed by a pause whilst the listeners come to terms with the number of years. Before they ask for any clarification I explain that the first cry I made was when my mother put me in the wicker basket and floated me down the Tamar. Having landed on the bank it now depends whether I am in Cornwall or Devon as to which bank I chose! Throughout the span of life, so far, I must confess that I am more concerned with losing my teeth than whether I am Cornish or Devonian. Both are important! No more so than teeth, a very important issue for all living in the southwest.

In fact it is the concern in the village of Whitehall. Here is the evidence:

Early in 2004 the West Country was devoid of any NHS dentists. Devon was one of the counties featured and because Exmouth had none at all, due to retirement and illness of the practicing team, I decided to write to our MP. Hugo Swire. Mr Swire replied at once informing me that he has raised an adjournment debate in Parliament to discuss the accessibility of NHS dentists in East Devon. He very kindly sent me a copy of a written verbatim account relative to the day and date of the debate. For reference it was headed 11 February 2004: column 454 WH. The following extract from Hansard gives relevant details:

'Scores of letters from concerned constituents extremely worried by the prospect of having to travel so far (inset-previously outlining current details of a round trip Exmouth to Cullompton costs £6 for an OAP – involving a 3 hours round trip) have promoted me to secure this debate. I have also received my first letter from a stalwart of Exmouth, the Exmouth Town Crier, the esteemed Tregarthen Gibson. He asked my help for the population of Exmouth, (being 34,000) which is, after all, Devon's largest town. Unless we get urgent extra dentistry in Exmouth, even Mr Tregarthen Gibson's teeth might be under threat. The prospect of a whimper rather than a cry from our Town Crier is too tragic to contemplate, but I digress'.

So do I! The few words in brackets and inset are mine, but do not deter or detract from the general theme and the factual work undertaken by our MP Hugo Swire. I am fortunate that in my humble position I often come into contact with him, and take this opportunity of thanking him for that which he has accomplished. The situation has improved and will no doubt, be solved. There is a more detailed account including the full quotation from Hansard.

From the sublime to the ridiculous, but it does happen! I refer to the ignominy of losing my false teeth in the sheer act of crying. There is nothing worse for the Crier, or indeed for the spectators than to see a gum exposed during the shout. Well perhaps there is! To be able visually to follow the path of said teeth through the air and onto the podium or dais on of which the unfortunate Crier is standing. Yet again the loss of teeth cannot take precedence over the tragic displacement of the clanger in the bell. It has suddenly decided without reference to anyone to give up its clang! It has been recorded that it has been known to drop on the way to the podium prior to the announcement of an Oyez! Nil point is the only result. What of the further embarrassment of losing ones feathers. Some, in order to adorn the tricorn hat worn traditionally by the Crier used decorative ostrich feathers, which, certainly in the southwest gale, flutter for from their peace aloft on the apex of a splendid figure dressed overall. There is nowhere that the ostrich can hide, or, for that matter the Town Crier.

12

NOSTALGLIA

In Delderfield's book *Exmouth Yesterdays* published in 1952 he speaks of street criers of vendors and intermittent craftsman street musicians. German bands were numerous, ump papa, ump papa! The organ grinder or hurdy-gurdy man and monkey. Later the Barrel Organ. The lamplighter or familiar figure, a taper burned on a long pole. One man band. Cornet players – trombone. Teams of three , bass drum, cornet, penny whistle. The violinist and ordinary vocalist. A sword swallower and jugglers on Chapel Hill. The strong man act. The humble pavement artist. Man with performing bear. Large field of fish vendors, Exe salmon. Hot chestnut man, 'warm your hands and fill your belly for a penny'. Ice cream sellers from highly decorated carts (hokey pokey hokey pokey penny a lump. That's the stuff to make you jump)'. Deango's chip carts 'my chips can be eaten but not beaten'. A chair mender, a knife grinder (windmills in exchange for jam jars). Rag and bone man wheeled his wheel barrow offering balloons and onion boys from Brittany on bicycles.

In those days (the book written in 1952 refers to late 1930s) one could always hear the strident tones of Jolly Whiddon, the Town Crier who drew attention to his presence by the ringing of a hand bell. Later he canvassed and bill posted for the dock companies steamer trips, and also up to the time of his death, sold the evening papers.

Fifty years later, how things have changed. But people? Their needs haven't. Life is about people and fifty years further on?

It'll be all the same, just the same,
A hundred years from now.
No use a' worrying, no use flurrying,
No use kicking up a row.
I shan't be here, you won't be here
When the hundred years have gone.
But somebody else will be well in the cart
And the world will still go on.

The coat of arms of Exmouth (left); emblazoned (right) on the shoulder of the author's regalia.

Exmouth is well documented and *Exmouth: Her Age Elegance* is the author's attempt to paint another picture of this interesting town.

A memory that will live long.
A close examination of the Exmouth town coat of arms will reveal that there are 2 lines of 5 ships making 10 in all. The embroidery on my cape, which is superb, and as you will recall is entirely the work of the ladies of Exmouth, is not only irreplaceable but also exquisitely fine. Fine in quality, fine in execution.

Should we close our eyes, we can remember that picture in detail and admire the execution of such beauty.

I had no cause to ask my audience to close their eyes. Many were blind, some partially sited, only the 'careers' who interpreted the phrases that I wish to emphasis, could help me. But the blind were more than capable. One lady ran her little finger over the sea scene, obviously counting the number of ships, minute when seen, that staggered me when she asked 'why are there only 10 ships?'. For once, I had no answer, only to admire the skill of the tactile sense, so able to reinforce what I had seen and know what was a total of 10. But it is only with this unique experience that one realises how fortunate most of us are to have the ability to see, and, perhaps be able to record the memorable event.

One of the duties of the Town Crier is to represent the town in many ways. I do, for example take part in a limited number of competitions and Town Criers contests. Aspects of these meetings I have details in another section of the book, but whilst mentioning these functions I would like to thank in particular the officers of the Ancient and Honourable Guild of Town Criers under whose rules we all participate and to individual town and other councils who have invited me to take part in their competitions. Included in this list are the following: Heart of England, a first for me held in Alcester, and Kingsbridge, Dartmouth, Yeovil, Topsham, Newton Abbot, Ilfracombe, and Witheridge where in 2005 I was awarded the Devon County Champion shield. It is another fact that there are a large number of Criers in Devon which underlines that in a rural community, they are necessary to disseminate information over a vast geographical part of the country.

However, the competitive nature of these gatherings is not necessarily me! Certainly, I take every opportunity of being involved and was delighted to represent Exmouth in the World Championship, held in Newquay Cornwall, in 2003. I had the advantage of performing in the county of my birth, completely at home with the accent and Cornish traditions and found myself in competition with over a hundred competitors and established that 'I was in a class of my own'. However, I returned to Exmouth to my extended family of 34,000. There is enough to do and enjoy in our lovely town, that, in its self is a full time occupation – so a decision has to be made. I'm usually very busy and always (well most of the time) content in my home town – Exmouth.

And so I continue in my present term of office, although nearing Mayor making day in May, the new Mayor might not ask me to continue, but appoint another. Meanwhile I have visited many voluntary bodies, groups, societies and will continue to do so. It gives me great pleasure, I can meet people in their choice of environment, congratulate the organisers for their expertise and enjoy myself, whether it be Line or Scottish dancing, polishing my computer skills or just rowing and getting no where on that punishing machine. I am so pleased when I receive an invitation, mainly in the winter months to give a talk on a range of subjects: 'A Funny Thing Happened To Me On The Way to the Office' (the meeting in the Church hall), or 'Trials and Tribulations and Yet The Joy Of Town Crying' – maybe 'From Author to Bell Ringer', 'From My Grotto with the Reindeer' – possibly, judging the 'impossible task' such as 127 Easter Bonnets and choosing the winner!

Ah well! Another term away from the children, although that's not accurate, I've had our family with us over the last holiday and its been a delight. But

Supporting the Poppy Appeal, 2002.

now I must make sure that my regalia is in pristine condition, lace cuffs and
jabot sparkle though the filigree made in Exmouth but named Honiton – a
neighbour. Another day has dawned.

13

THE WELFARE OF THE TOWN CRIER

Sometime in the middle eighties (that's 1980!) I was referred by a well liked and well-known GP Dr Stephen Price, to the Exmouth Sports Centre to undertake a Pulse course. Due to a hiccup in health and a very irregular heart beat, it was necessary for me to follow this course of action. It was fortunate that facilities exist in Exmouth for this treatment. P.U.L.S.E. is a most interesting and successful initiative, under the direction of Andy Reay, the Manager, of an expanding and well developed establishment. A team of young dedicated informed staff who encouraged the patients to help themselves ensure that the facilities at the centre were efficiently used.

Over twenty-five years later I am still on the list of those who attend platform one, as it is now known, to exercise according to regulations laid down initially by my GP. Furthermore, I enjoy the period of training, felt much better within myself, far more comfortable with the movement necessary to establish and enjoy that comfort.

I was, therefore, interested in a scheme designed by a team of enthusiasts not in a specialist field of medical aid but in a combination of physical activity and social contact. The outcome was ' Devon – Walk This Way'. A group of people drawn together medically by their doctors and by adding the social side themselves accepted the opportunity to walk and have a chat.

In Exmouth, two groups have for several years now been getting together either on Tuesday or Saturday morning in walking on a short, level, voluntary walk which according to the participants by their own admission and their repetition of their chosen activity seem to derive some benefit physically or socially.

I have, by invitation of Devon/E.D.D.C. representatives who set up the scheme joined in a number of the walks in good and not so good weather and shared a cheery smile, an exchange of ideas and at the same time gaining some benefit from the fresh air and sunshine. A word of thanks to those who are in anyway responsible for the provision of the scheme and to those who have volunteered to assist in the supervision of such groups. This takes the form of documentation, i.e. an attendance register, choice of route and general overseeing that the individual members are not being hurried or over taxed by any enthusiasts. What was it in the distant past of army manoeuvres? Take the time of the slowest and leave no-one in distress.

There are many of the former and more of the later in the Tuesday or Saturday Walk This Way Group. Would you like to join them? Would you care to volunteer as an assistant? Its simple, its free, its beneficial, pleasant and self motivated and finally – fun!

As a postscript - it is advisable to take a few coins with you – it has been known for some to partake of party activity and although 3-course meals are not on the menu, teas, coffee, chocolate and soft drinks are usually the favourites.

Meet at Manor Gardens at 10.15am for 10.30am start on Tuesdays and Saturdays at the information centre Manor Gardens. Go on have a go! I first wrote this invitation in May 2002 an article in the *Journal* entitled 'You'll Never Forget It', and we haven't!

The Walk This Way Team - false start!

APPENDIX 1

EXMOUTH'S COAT OF ARMS RETURN FROM LIMBO

In October 1997, Exmouth Town Council was granted the use of the town's Coat of Arms which had remained out of use since 1974 when the old Exmouth Urban District Council was abolished. As Exmouth did not have a council of its own after 1974, with most functions transferred to East Devon District Council, there was not local authority to which the right to use the arms could pass.

With the creation of a Town Council for Exmouth in 1996 that situation was put right and the new Council applied to have the arms transferred. Such matters are dealt with by the Royal College of Arms and require an Order placed before Parliament. This was done in the Autumn of 1997, presented and approved at the Court of Buckingham Palace on 30 October and came into effect on 29 November 1997. From that date, the right to use the Coat of Arms belongs to Exmouth Town Council.

The Coat of Arms was originally granted to the Exmouth Urban District Council on 12th February 1947. It consists of three parts - the Shield, the Crest (above the shield) and the motto. Officially, the Arms are described as follows:

> *Argent two anchors in saltire gules between four fish naiant azure on a chief of the last ten ancient ships in full sail five and five of the field. And for the Crest issuant from a mural crown argent and between two magnoliae grandiflorae Exmouthiensis proper a tower or thereon a flagstaff proper flying therefrom to the sinister a flag also argent charged with a cross gules with mantling azure doubled argent.*

In plain English, the Arms represent selected aspects of the town's history. The anchors depict the association with the Royal Navy (through the Royal Marines and ships bearing the name HMS *Exmouth*). The fish denote the local fishing industry. The ships commemorate the ten ships and 193 seamen contributed from Exmouth to the fleet setting out for the siege of Calais under Edward VIII in 1346. The 'mural coronet' (sitting on top of the helmet) represents a local authority and the tower rising from it depicts the fort at the mouth of the Exe defended by Royalists in 1646. The banner of St George flies from the tower.

The leaves and flowers are of the Magnolia 'Grandiflora Exmouthiensis', first brought to England by Sir John Colleton from America. Sir John died in 1754 and is buried at St Michael's Burial Ground at Withycombe Raleigh.

The motto: 'Mare ditat flores decorani' means 'the Sea enriches, the flowers adorn'.

The Coat of Arms may only be fifty years old, but it represents a proud history stretching back least six hundred and fifty years. And now, after twenty-two years gathering dust, Exmouth can once again show off its Coat of Arms and all it represents.

APPENDIX 2
REPRESENTING EXMOUTH

My very first competition with the Ancient and Honourable Guild of Town Criers was in the 'Hearts of England' competition in Alcester, followed over the years by appearances in Kingsbridge, Dartmouth, Yeovil Topsham, Newton Abbot, Witheridge and Ilfracombe. Devon is fortunate in having more Town Criers than any other county and I have received invitations to attend events from as far afield as Bromyard, Peterborough, Hatherleigh, Tavistock and Blandford Forum which, for various reasons, I have had to decline. While socially very desirable, and while I wish Exmouth to be represented as often as possible, these events do take up an enormous amount of time, and the competitive nature of these sessions is not necessarily me! I prefer to spend time with my family of 34,000 and rising in Exmouth. Here there is more than enough to occupy my time as the following list of events and visits indicates:

I continue to visit as many voluntary bodies, groups, societies and activities as possible including: Heritage Walks, The Blue Plaque Trail, Walk this Way (for those who can take little or no exercise), Music and Arts Festivals, Women's Institutes, Probus and Rotary Clubs, Townswomen's Guilds, Carnival Fun Days, The Annual Illuminated Carnival, Christmas Charity Cards for good causes, Friends of the Hospital, branches of the Royal British Legion, fêtes and functions, Exmouth Library events, art exhibitions, Friendship Force (USA), opening of new public houses, garden clubs, sand sculptures, light exhibitions, refurbished establishments, Twinning Associations, Civic Receptions (Exmouth is twinned with Langerwehe in Germany and Dinan in France and I have visited both).

Other events, occasions and appointments include Business South West at Westpoint, President of the Exmouth Society, visits in support of Devon Wildlife Trust, Centre Stage (Youth Drama Group), Exe Valley Support Group, British Heart Foundation, Devon Air Ambulance Trust, Youth Council, Town Concert Band, Wards and Staff at Exmouth Hospital, South West Band Festival, Remembrance Days, various fêtes, visits to the elderly to Widecombe-in-the-Moor with the Rotary Club, Children In Need, Adventure Trust for Girls, Phoenix Friendship Group, Sing-a-long with Primary and Infant Schools, Radio and TV shows in Devon, Christmas illuminations, Mayor's Annual Charity Civic Ball, Exmouth Traders and Shopkeepers activities, Christmas Santa's Grotto 2004, Open Door Centre, late night shopping events, Christmas Fun Fairs, Third Age Project, 41 Club, Former Orcombeleigh MS Holiday Home, Children's Hospice South West, Coast Watch Station, birthday celebrations for people of all ages (often for those in care, and for those celebrating special occasions), births, marriages and deaths, The Summer Festival (often 10 days, now known as Exmouth Festival arranged through two Bank Holidays in May), Hospicecare, the Town Management Forum and associated groups - Marketing and Tourism, the Museum, Young People's Drama, The Blackmore Theatre, the Tidy Group, Performance Stage Programme, Home Start, R.M.C. at Lympstone, Stroke Club, Cinnamon Trust, Beach Rescue, Exmouth Operatic Society, Devon and Dorset Regiment, 531st tribute celebrations including HMS *Exmouth* - memories and celebrations, children's visit to Crealy Park by taxi owners in co-operation with Exmouth Rotarians, Leisure Centre, Exmouth Waterfront Project, Victorian Garden fêtes at Manor Lodge, close association with Morton House and other residential homes, students studying English from Italy, visiting the Town Hall, local government, Age Concern in all its aspects, Littleham Fun event, ceramics at Kennaway Centre, Continuing Education Courses, Exmouth Photo Group, Moose, International Fete, annual Exmouth Hospital fête, flower festivals in each of the main churches in the town, new nursery at Littleham Primary School, Exmouth Art Group annual exhibition, The Lions Fete, Residents' Association, Rainbow Project, RNLI in all its aspects throughout town and country, Town and Gown - links with Rolle College, association with Rag Week (including the 'kidnap' for Children In Need as reported elsewhere in this book).

Along with this I have been Master of Ceremonies at numerous events, visited as Town Crier those towns without their own (Lympstone, Sidmouth, Budleigh Salterton, National Federation of Post Office and BT Pensioners, Exmouth Gallery (children's art, sculpture garden, display of work in Community as well as in the gallery sponsored by the Town Council), involvement in the Gateway to the Jurassic Coast project. Then there's the Swimming, Life Saving and Beach Safety Groups, not forgetting bowls, cricket, football, rowing and rugby, along with many other sporting activities. Along with these are singing groups and choirs. Wessex Trains have added support and sponsorship to many local projects, especially to the Exmouth Festival in 2004/5. Of all these events, occasions and associations none is more important than the Exmouth Club for the Blind and Partially Sighted, including links with the Talking Newspaper.

Finally I am most proud to have been able to record the history of our growing and thriving town in my earlier book *Exmouth - Her Age of Elegance*.

APPENDIX 3
LETTERS OF THANKS AND APPRECIATION

EXMOUTH BEACH RESCUE CLUB

Founded: 1986

Club Colours: Yellow
Dk Blue
Lt Blue

President: J Taylor Esq

Reg Charity No. 1025654

Kevin Gulbranson-Brown
40 Capel Lane
Exmouth
Devon
EX8 2QZ

Mr Tregarthen Gibson
The Town Crier of Exmouth
Dolforgan Court
Louisa Terrace
Exmouth
Devon
EX8 2AQ

24th February 2004

Dear Mr Tregarthen Gibson,

Thank you very much for the £10 donation received via yourself from the Exmouth Townswomen Guild. The Exmouth Beach Rescue Club very much appreciates your support, and every donation received contributes towards the clubs activities allowing us to continue a valuable service.

Yours sincerely,

Kevin Gulbranson-Brown.

(Secretary, Exmouth Beach Rescue Club)

Lifeboats
Royal National Lifeboat Institution

Royal National Lifeboat Institution
Registered charity number 209603
Supported entirely by voluntary contributions
Patron: Her Majesty The Queen
President: HRH The Duke of Kent KG
Chairman: Peter Nicholson

From:
Exmouth & Budleigh Salterton Guild

FROM
MRS. M. CHANDLER
20 PORTLAND AVE, EXMOUTH, DEVON EX8 2BS
TEL. 01395 278821

Mr. G.Gibson
Dolforgan Court
Exmouth
Devon EX8

3rd April 2004

Dear Garth

This letter is to acknowledge a cheque for £25.00. that Keith Graham has recently handed to me as a fundraising donation. I understand you gave a talk and donated the money to the R.N.L.I. thank you very much.

Enclosed is an official receipt for your records.

Also enclosed is our latest newsletter and a list of our events planned so far for 2004, if you can advertise any of them when the time arrives that would be very much appreciated. You are always welcome to attend any of our events.

Thanks once again.

Kind regards

Maureen

Maureen Chandler
Hon. Sec. Fundraising Guild

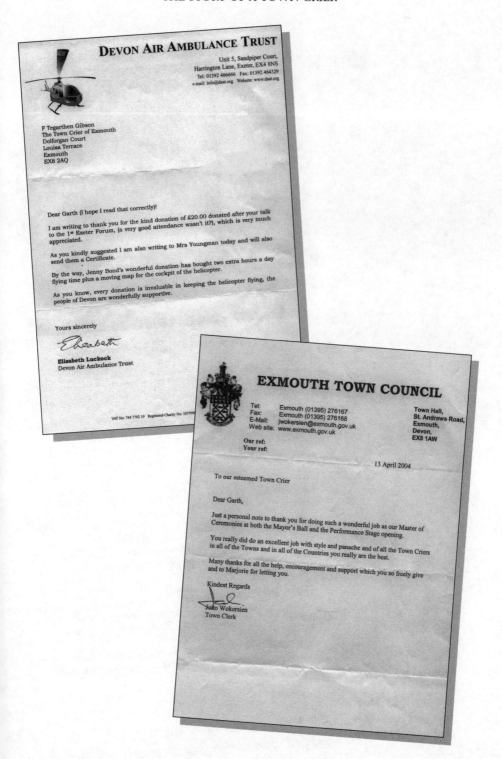

DEVON AIR AMBULANCE TRUST

Unit 5, Sandpiper Court,
Harrington Lane, Exeter, EX4 8NS
Tel: 01392 466666 Fax: 01392 464329
e-mail: info@daat.org Website: www.daat.org

F Tegarthen Gibson
The Town Crier of Exmouth
Dolforgan Court
Louisa Terrace
Exmouth
EX8 2AQ

Dear Garth (I hope I read that correctly)!

I am writing to thank you for the kind donation of £20.00 donated after your talk
to the 1st Exeter Forum, (a very good attendance wasn't it?), which is very much
appreciated.

As you kindly suggested I am also writing to Mrs Youngman today and will also
send them a Certificate.

By the way, Jenny Bond's wonderful donation has bought two extra hours a day
flying time plus a moving map for the cockpit of the helicopter.

As you know, every donation is invaluable in keeping the helicopter flying, the
people of Devon are wonderfully supportive.

Yours sincerely

Elisabeth

Elisabeth Luckock
Devon Air Ambulance Trust

VAT No: 744 7702 19 Registered Charity No: 1077998

EXMOUTH TOWN COUNCIL

Tel: Exmouth (01395) 276167
Fax: Exmouth (01395) 276168
E-Mail: jwokersien@exmouth.gov.uk
Web site: www.exmouth.gov.uk

Town Hall,
St. Andrews Road,
Exmouth,
Devon,
EX8 1AW

Our ref:
Your ref:

13 April 2004

To our esteemed Town Crier

Dear Garth,

Just a personal note to thank you for doing such a wonderful job as our Master of
Ceremonies at both the Mayor's Ball and the Performance Stage opening.

You really did an excellent job with style and panache and of all the Town Criers
in all of the Towns and in all of the Countries you really are the best.

Many thanks for all the help, encouragement and support which you so freely give
and to Marjorie for letting you.

Kindest Regards

John Wokersien
Town Clerk

105

Royal Beacon Hotel

10 March 2004

Mr F. Tregarthen Gibson
Dolforgan Court
Louisa Terrace
Exmouth
EX8 2AQ

Dear Garth

I must first apologise for not getting back to you sooner, only I seem to be getting busier and busier, even after our 'New Beginning' launch.

I just wish that busier and busier went hand in hand with profit - it doesn't!

Thank you so much for your splendid appearance and management of the latter part of our open day; there is no doubt that your presence gave the whole affair a more formal and 'proper' sense of occasion.

I have had so many kind comments from so many people and I do feel that we put on, what some would say, a really good show.

I look forward to seeing you again, and thank you once again for your excellent performance.

Yours sincerely and
with kind regards

Paul Nightingale

Exmouth Twinning Association

Mr J Wokeriein
Town Clerk
Exmouth Town Council

2 August 2004

Dear Sir,

On behalf of the Association, I am writing to express our thanks and appreciation for the civic welcome extended to the visitors from our twin town of Langerwehe on Friday 23 July. Everyone who attended has said that the buffet provided was excellent and we would like you to pass our compliments on to the Manager and staff of the Manor Hotel.

Our sincere thanks also to the Deputy Mayor, Councillor Eileen Wragg, who gave a great welcome speech. The Community hope that she and her husband enjoyed the evening meal and dance at the Pavilion.

Also please give our thanks to Garth Gibson and the excellent volunteers of the Blue Plaque Brigade, who gave us all, visitors and residents alike an enjoyable walk and history lesson.

Once again our great thanks and I look forward to arranging the visit from Dinan in 2005 with you and your excellent staff.

Yours sincerely,

Frank Payne
Secretary

Goosewing Cottage
Staplake Road
Starcross
Devon
EX6 8PQ

Exmouth Town Council
Council Chambers
St. Andrews Road
Exmouth
Devon   *7 May 2003*

Dear Sir/Madam

Exmouth Town Crier

On Saturday 26 April 2003, a family of four from St Lambert Du Lattay (twinned with Kenton) in the Loire Valley came to stay with us in Starcross for four days. It was their first visit to England .

As the weather was sunny, we decided to catch the ferry from Starcross to Exmouth – a very pleasant boat trip. Having arrived safely on foreign shores in Exmouth, we meandered through your beautiful gardens where we had the very good fortune to meet your Town Crier. As he approached us, he immediately engaged us in conversation and when I explained that our friends were visitors from France he immediately conversed with them and had his photograph taken with them on the green. He then rang his bell and did an 'Oh Ye' 'Oh Ye' and announced their arrival from France. This really made the day for them!

I am writing to you because I believe that your Town Crier is a real ambassador for Exmouth. He went out of his way to make our French visitors extremely welcome and even welcomed us from across the waters in Starcross and for this I am extremely grateful.

Well done Exmouth you should indeed be proud of your town Crier- he is a real asset to you – we will certainly venture over the water again to see you!

Yours faithfully,

Liz Hicks

INNER WHEEL CLUB OF EXMOUTH

Dear Garth,

We enjoyed your visit to our Inter Club so much and as a result of your generosity our treasurer has been able to send a cheque for £95 to our Association Presidents charity – Cystic Fibrosis Trust.

I knew nothing about this charity until our Association Conference this year, when one of the speaker was Nicky West and her words really moved me. Aged 29 and dying from this disease that she has inherited.

My year as President is just ending, and I must tell you that the afternoon that you entertained us so well will remain one of the highlights of my year in office.

Thanks again,

Rosemary Weigold

32 Winchester Road
Eccles
Manchester
M30 9BU

Town Hall
Exmouth
EX8 1AW

Dear Mr Town Crier,

Enclosed copies of photo's taken in your town centre. May I say thankyou for your time and cheerful words. Us four ladies spent a week in Exmouth, we found it a beautiful clean place and all the people we met were friendly and kind.

Bless you,

Sandra Harris

I am the one with white hair and I'm the youngest!

POSTSCRIPT

Vic Garth, Town Crier.

A MESSAGE FROM MELVA STOTT, QUEENSLAND, AUSTRALIA

Maybe it's fortunate that there are no town criers in Greece. Their national anthem has 158 verses – it's even slightly longer than South Africa's.

We have just returned from Tasmania after attending the funeral of Vice Garth in Hobart. He was 92 and virtually died with his bell in his hand as he was doing his town crying rounds (albeit in a wheelchair) until shortly before his death. The only other crier to attend was James Carter, who read a message from Tony Evans. Stan Cried on behalf of the Australian Guild, and I read a poem that I had written on the way to the ferry and called 'The Padre's Bell'.

Saturday 11 December 2004
Campbell Street, Hobart, Tasmania

Peter Higgins – Chairman of The Exmouth Society and his wife Hilary sent me this photograph of 'Vic' aged 92 and a half years, the Town Crier of Hobart, and the oldest Town Crier in Tasmania.

The occasion was The Annual Tasmanian Motorcycle Charity Ride, which provides toys for children's charities. There were 7,400 motorbikes taking part and they took 30-45 minutes to pass by. Here is an extract from the *Sunday Tasmanian* from 12 December 2004:

'From the roar of Harleys to the buzz of Vespas, 7400 motorbikes from all parts of the state clogged Hobart's streets yesterday as the Motorcycle Riders Association Christmas Toy Run hit town.

While other motorists may have been inconvenienced, most took the delays in the spirit of the season. Police were out in force to make sure the strict safety guidelines for the event were followed. Event organiser Chris Cook said there were few mishaps:

'Overall I am very happy and I'm sure if there were any problems the police would have handled it,' he said.

Thousands of toys were given to the Salvation Army for distribution – enough to fill three trucks and a trailer.'

I am told that Vic had to be prompted by his daughter to ring his bell!

The postcard is of Vic as a younger (and fitter) Town Crier in Salamanca Market, Hobart, which is the largest outdoor market in Australia. As the opening to this postcript reports, Vic has since died but one hopes that Hobart will continue its tradition of Town Crier.

On a personal note, I have no idea of the age of the oldest Town Crier in this country, but I feel 90+ sometimes. No! I'm not even approaching that figure at the moment, but would be interested to hear, maybe through 'The Crier' for a possible mention in the Guinness Book of Records. To answer the request I will qualify as an octogenarian – soon! It really depends upon the publication date of this book.

AND FINALLY!

FROM A REPORT IN THE EXPRESS & ECHO NEWSPAPER, SEPT. 2005

The Town Crier of Exmouth does have plenty to shout about after winning the Devon Town Crier's Championship. Crowned Champion of Devon on 13 September 2005, Tregarthen Gibson swept the board at Witheridge, near Tiverton. His last appearance was at Newton Abbot for the 9 Guild Competition organised under the auspices of the Ancient and Honourable Guild of Town Criers.

Garth, as he is known, resplendent in blue and gold, and tricorn, lace and buckles, received a shield as county winner at his first attempt, since becoming the resort's town crier in 2000. Prior to this year, the date at Witheridge always clashed with the Exmouth Festival and his duty and commitment was to his home town.

However, when asked about the Devon Competition he said ' It is gratifying to win a competition of this calibre and I'm delighted to be able to play my part in putting Exmouth firmly on the map.'

Garth was congratulated at Exmouth Town Council's meeting, and the Mayor, Councillor Eileen Wragg, said: 'Garth is a wonderful town character and he rightly deserves our praise and thanks.'

Town Manager, John Furze, when asked to comment confirmed the A.H.G.T.C. involvement in development of the competition and encouraged groups to up-hold the traditional pastimes to ensure that Devon was one of the strongest and well-represented county for criers.

Tregarthen Gibson of Exmouth can now look forward to further success having joined the celebrated group of Town Criers throughout Devon.

To JOHN WOKERSIEN, Town Clerk,

John,
You will be pleased to know that on Saturday 25th June 2005 The Devon County Championship of Town Criers was held at Witheridge in Mid Devon by a Charter dated 1210 to hold a Fair of St Johns in the town. The competition was organised under the rules and regulations laid down by the Ancient and Honourable Guild of Town Criers. I am delighted to inform you, and ask whether Council should be informed by The Mayor that 'Tregarthen of Exmouth' is the Devon County Champion 2005.

Previous holders of the prestigious award, only open to the Town Criers of Devon, include Kingsbridge, Cullompton, Topsham, Dawlish, Dartmouth, Ilfracombe and now in 2005 Exmouth! During the last five years I have attended competitions in each of these towns, except Chumleigh and Dawlish, but this year, due to the change of dates of our Festival, I was able to attend the Devon Championships and add the name of Exmouth to the Trophy Shield.

I am proud that I was given the opportunity to compete and win! I have in the past visited- other competitions, including Yeovil, Heart of England in Alcester, The World Championships held in 2003 in Newquay, Cornwall which included European competitors in addition to those from Canada, USA and Australia. The latter is hosting this year's World Championship. I always wish to have Exmouth represented, but time is the limiting factor in my commitment to Exmouth - the largest town in the county, without adding the continents of the New World. I am content to do my part, but it is so encouraging for Exmouth to WIN!

Sincerely,

F Tregarthen Gibson
Town Crier - 'Tregarthen of Exmouth'

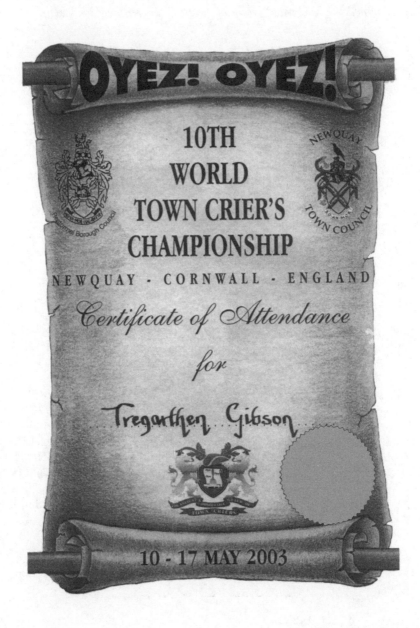